What is economics?

Economics is the study of how goods and services are produced, distributed, and consumed by society. Because resources are usually assumed to be in short supply, the field was described by English economist Lionel Robbins in 1935 as "the science of scarcity".

The word "economics" was coined from the Greek words **oikos** (household) and **nomos** (law), so it means something like household rule or home management.

Though "household" is now generalized to include individuals, companies, countries, and the entire world system.

While people have been calling themselves professional economists only since the 19th century, the field has roots that go back much further.

MAN SHOT BY WIFE

Old money

Economic thought is at least as old as money itself.

The earliest coins were made from precious metals such as gold and silver. They are believed to have first appeared around the 6th century BC in what is now Turkey, but were soon in use around the civilized world, from Mesopotamia to Persia to India to China.

We therefore begin our story 2,500 years ago, in a cave in ancient Greece …

→ **INTRODUCING**

ECONOMICS

DAVID ORRELL & BORIN VAN LOON

Published in the UK and the USA
in 2011 by Icon Books Ltd,
Omnibus Business Centre,
39–41 North Road, London N7 9DP
email: info@iconbooks.com
www.introducingbooks.com

Sold in the UK, Europe and Asia
by Faber & Faber Ltd,
Bloomsbury House,
74–77 Great Russell Street,
London WC1B 3DA or their agents

Distributed in South Africa
by Jonathan Ball,
Office B4, The District,
41 Sir Lowry Road,
Woodstock 7925

Distributed in Australia and
New Zealand by Allen & Unwin Pty Ltd,
PO Box 8500,
83 Alexander Street,
Crows Nest, NSW 2065

Distributed to the trade in the USA
by Consortium Book Sales
and Distribution
The Keg House,
34 Thirteenth Avenue NE, Suite 101,
Minneapolis, MN 55413-1007

Distributed in Canada
by Penguin Books Canada,
90 Eglinton Avenue East,
Suite 700, Toronto,
Ontario M4P 2Y3

ISBN: 978-184831-215-9

Edited by Duncan Heath

Printed by Clays Ltd, St Ives plc

EG SO215

Pythagoras

The philosopher **Pythagoras** (c. 570–c. 495 BC) is today associated mostly with mathematics, and his famous theorem about right-angled triangles that we all learn at school. But he has had a lasting influence on science in general, including economics.

Pythagoras was considered a demi-god by the Greeks. His birth was predicted by the oracle at Delphi, and it was rumoured that his father was the god Apollo.

His school grew into what amounts to a pseudo-religious cult, based on the worship of **number**. The Pythagoreans were highly secretive and left no written documents, so we only know about them indirectly.

Harmony of the Spheres

The Pythagoreans believed that all things were composed of number. Each number had a special, almost magical significance. The most sacred number was 10, which was symbolized by the tetractys.

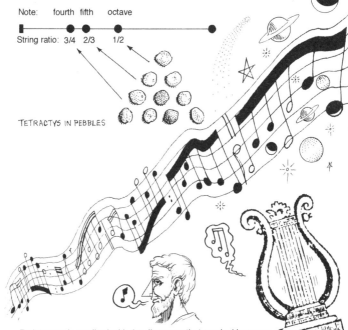

Note: fourth fifth octave

String ratio: 3/4 2/3 1/2

TETRACTYS IN PEBBLES

Pythagoras is credited with the discovery that musical harmony is based on numerical ratios between string lengths. Because music was considered to be the most mysterious of art forms, this backed up the belief that the entire cosmos was based on number: what the Pythagoreans called the Harmony of the Spheres.

Economics, and money itself, are also based on the Pythagorean idea that all things can be reduced to number. Indeed, it is believed that Pythagoras was involved in introducing the first coinage to his region.

*O*ikonomikos

The word "economics" was derived from a work by the philosopher **Xenophon** (431– c. 360 BC), who was influenced by Pythagoras. His tract *Oikonomikos* described how to efficiently organize and run an agricultural estate.

> It must, I should think, be the business of the good estate manager at any rate to manage his own house or estate well.

He argued that complicated tasks could best be carried out through division of labour. An advantage of cities such as Athens, which was growing rapidly in size and complexity, was the availability of a variety of specialists. In smaller towns, people had to carry out more tasks themselves, which was less efficient.

While this conclusion predated Adam Smith's thoughts on the same topic by a couple of millennia (see p. 60), in a slave-based society the coordinating of these specialists was a task for the estate manager, not the markets.

Plato's *Republic*

Plato (427–347 BC) took the idea of an optimally-managed estate a step further with his *Republic*, which described a utopian society ruled over by philosopher kings known as "guardians".

To safeguard against corruption, the guardians will not be allowed to own property or lay their hands on gold or silver, and will receive only a basic living wage.

Their interest will therefore be for the wealth of the society as a whole, not themselves.

Every task, including the raising of children, would be allocated to specialists. Property would be divided according to mathematical principles. The maximum number of citizens was computed by Plato to be 5,040, which has the property that it is divisible by the numbers 1 through 10 and so can be easily divided into separate administrative groups.

ristotle

Plato's most famous student was **Aristotle** (384–322 BC), who wrote and taught on subjects ranging from astronomy to medicine to ethics. He believed that the sole purpose of money was to act as a medium for exchange. As he wrote in *Nichomachean Ethics*, 'all things are measured by money'.

According to Aristotle, the fair distribution of goods could be determined by different mathematical formulae, known as the Pythagorean means.

For example, suppose that one person wants to sell a piece of land to another. The seller wants at least 120 currency units, but the buyer wants to pay at most 80.

In this case the correct price will be the **harmonic mean**, which is 96. This number is 20 per cent more than the lower price, but 20 per cent less than the higher price.

Just as music was governed by number, so was the idea of just distribution.

$\mathcal{A}$ system of opposites

In his *Metaphysics*, Aristotle attributes the following list of opposites to the Pythagoreans (who being highly secretive did not let it out themselves):

Limited	Unlimited
Odd	Even
One	Plurality
Right	Left
Male	Female
At rest	In motion
Straight	Crooked
Light	Darkness
Square	Oblong
Good	Evil

The Pythagoreans associated the left column with good, and the right column with evil. This list has been influential on the course of Western scientific thought, and therefore on economics.

Limited vs. unlimited

For example, the idea of limits was important to the Greeks, including Aristotle.

Aristotle noticed that merchants often accumulated immense amounts of money just through exchange, even though they did not produce anything themselves. In *Politics*, he therefore distinguished between two types of exchange.

The second, unnatural, type of exchange occurred when goods were exchanged for the sole purpose of making money. Usury (lending money for interest) was particularly unethical, since it allows money to grow without limit, violating the bounds of nature.

Spreading the word

Aristotle, like Plato, was a teacher. One of his students was a young man by the name of Alexander – a military genius who would go on to conquer an area stretching from Egypt to part of India.

After the collapse of Alexander the Great's empire in the 3rd century BC, Western economic thought went into something of a deep freeze. The teachings of Aristotle and other Greek thinkers remained locked away in the libraries.

The Dark Ages

The Romans were more interested in building viaducts than holding economics seminars. However, they did make huge contributions in the development of a legal system, including the protection of property rights which underpins capitalism.*

The fall of the Roman empire has been blamed on many factors, but the economy was certainly one of them.

In the 3rd century AD, the lack of new foreign conquests meant the supply of precious metals decreased.

Coins were therefore debased, resulting in severe inflation.

The Dark Ages

Rome's decline was followed by the period that came to be known as the Dark Ages, though today historians prefer to call it the Early Middle Ages (roughly from the 5th century AD to the 11th century). Trade and the importance of towns declined, and the economy was based largely on self-sufficiency.

* Capitalism is an economic system based on private ownership of the means of production and trading goods for profit.

The Middle Ages

Economic thought in the Middle Ages was dominated by religion, and in particular the battle between Christianity and Islam. The focus was on ethics.

The Old Testament contained many statements about the economy. It forbade usury, and in the "Jubilee" every seven years, all debts were to be cancelled. The rewards of hard work were considered just, but the pursuit of wealth for its own sake was discouraged.

The New Testament took a more directly anti-business line – perhaps because the imminent second coming of Christ meant the end of the world in its current form. This made the pursuit of wealth a little redundant.

The growth of Islam

What Europeans call the Dark Ages was a bright age for Islam. It was marked by the Muslim conquest of Arabia, North Africa, Persia, and parts of Spain. Increasing trade meant there was great interest in the role of money, which was by then far more widely used.

As with the Christian Bible, the Koran included statements that applied to the economy. Again, usury was forbidden.

And poor people should be supported through the proceeds of taxation.

The Muslim scholar known in Europe as **Averroes** (Ibn Rushd, 1126–98) was born in Cordoba, Spain. His work encompassed many areas, including law, astronomy, and translating Aristotle.

While Aristotle saw money as a somewhat arbitrary means of exchange and measure of value, Averroes believed that money, like Allah, was fixed and unchangeable. It was therefore a sin for a ruler to dilute its value, for example by reducing the precious metal content of coins.

Feudalism

Christian Europe was organized in a rigidly hierarchical system now known as feudalism.

The largest and most powerful landlord was the Church. In concert with religious orders like the Knights Templar,* the system was successful at generating military power – very important in a time when land was usually acquired through conquest rather than a real estate office, and the expression "hostile takeover" could be taken literally.

Christian Europe eventually recaptured much of the territory it had lost to the Muslims. This led to a huge expansion in the size of their trade routes and economy. Through the translations of Averroes, Aristotle was rediscovered.

* During the Crusades, the Knights Templar set up the world's first banks.

The universities

In the 12th century, growing prosperity, an emerging class of city-dwellers, and the rediscovery of ancient thinkers all led to an interest in learning. People suddenly had a need for higher education. But to satisfy it, they needed to invent a new institution: the university.

The first recognized universities were in Bologna (1088), Paris (c. 1150), and Oxford (1167).

Others quickly followed, and by the beginning of the 15th century there were over 50 universities across Europe, all controlled by the Catholic Church.

At the centre of the curriculum were the works of Aristotle. A school of economic thought now known as **Scholastic economics**, based in Paris, aimed to reconcile Aristotle's ideas about money and property with Christian theology.

Saint Thomas Aquinas

This synthesis of Aristotelian and Christian doctrines reached its highest point with the Dominican friar **Thomas Aquinas** (1225–74), who taught in Paris and Cologne. Aquinas put great emphasis on the rationality of Greek philosophy.

Reason in man is rather like God in the world.

His concept of a "just price" corresponded to the conventionally-accepted price that would hold when neither the buyer nor the seller were under duress. Aquinas allowed that the price for a good could be agreed between two parties by haggling, but it was unjust for one party to take advantage of the other – for example by charging a starving person more during a famine.

Copernicus

One of Aristotle's teachings was that the Sun rotated around the Earth. This idea was warmly endorsed by the Church, since in their interpretation it put God's greatest creations – ourselves – at the centre of the cosmos. In the 16th century, however, the Polish astronomer **Copernicus** (1473–1543) disturbed this Aristotelian/Christian worldview by pointing out, in a text published just before his death, that it would be much simpler, at least in a mathematical, Pythagorean kind of way, if we assumed instead that the Earth rotated around the Sun.

On a less controversial level, Copernicus also advised the King of Poland on how to maintain a currency.

It is my conclusion that money usually depreciates when it becomes too abundant.

This is perhaps the first statement of what is now known as the quantity theory of money.

Navarrus

Copernicus's words were echoed by the Dominican priest **Navarrus** (1493–1586), based at Salamanca in Spain.

All merchandise becomes dearer when it is in strong demand and short supply.

Money, in so far as it may be sold, bartered, or exchanged by some other form of contract, is merchandise and therefore also becomes dearer when it is in great demand and short supply.

While money was still considered an essentially sterile means of exchange, it also had a dynamic of its own. This insight was particularly relevant, given the massive amount of gold that was starting to find its way into Spain from New World mines, thanks to the efforts of the Conquistadores.

Mercantilism

Medieval Scholastic economics focused on small-scale transactions between individuals (microeconomics) and was dominated by monks who had taken a vow of poverty. By the time of the Renaissance (14th to 17th centuries), attention was shifting from the micro to the macro; and from questions of ethics to how to make money.

The feudal system was being replaced by centralized and militarily powerful nation states headed by monarchies. Technological advances in shipping, and expeditions by Columbus and other explorers, led to the opening up of valuable new trade routes in America and Asia and an explosion in world trade. Restrictions on usury were gradually relaxed. A political and economic movement known as **mercantilism** emerged, dedicated to building and maintaining the reach and power of nations.

Gold is a wonderful thing! Whoever possesses it is master of everything he desires.

The rise of empire

The first economy to fully organize itself along mercantilist lines was England under Queen Elizabeth I. Her naval fleet would eventually allow the British empire to become the largest in history. Other Western powers, particularly Spain and France, weren't far behind.

According to mercantilism, the world economy was a game played by nation states; and its objective was to win as much "treasure" as possible, in the form of gold and silver. In countries without gold and silver mines, like England, this was accomplished through trade, conquest, and hard labour – supplied in part by colonial slaves.

The total amount of wealth in the world was assumed to be fixed, so the economy was a zero-sum game. As the English businessman/economist **Thomas Mun** (1571–1641) put it:

Page 22

Mercantilist economics

In place of monastic scholars or philosophers, the new economic ideas were developed by multi-talented Renaissance men, including public officials, journalists, and businessmen like Mun, who was a director of the East India Company.

Mercantilist economists did not aim to describe an overarching theory of the economy or moral behaviour, but focused instead on individual technical issues such as trade or currency.

They argued that the government should use trade tariffs, monopolies and subsidies to encourage exports, thus bringing money into the country, and discourage imports. Military power was essential to find and control new resources.

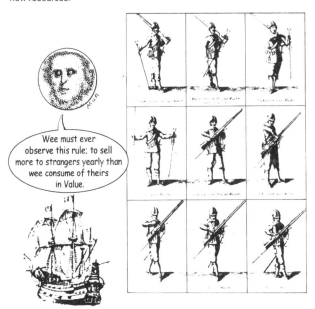

Wee must ever observe this rule; to sell more to strangers yearly than wee consume of theirs in Value.

$\mathcal{P}$ower of the state

Maintaining an empire was expensive, so governments were constantly having to raise funds. They also suffered from other domestic problems, such as inflation (caused, as Navarrus had predicted, by the expansion of money supply) and poverty, brought about by the breakdown of the medieval social structure. As Queen Elizabeth noted: "Paupers are everywhere!"

In 1601 she introduced the Elizabethan Poor Law to help out. However, economists generally adopted a Machiavellian approach to the economy. The aim was to maximize the power of the state.

As **Jean-Baptiste Colbert** (1619–83), Minister of Finance under King Louis XIV of France, asserted:

It is simply, and solely, the abundance of money within a state that makes the difference in its grandeur and power.

Strength in numbers

A large working class was essential to provide manpower and an internal market. As the English writer and journalist **Daniel Defoe** (1659–1731) noted:

People are indeed the essential of commerce, and ...

the more people the more trade;

... the more trade, the more money;

... the more money, the more strength;

... and the more strength, the greater the nation.

The purpose of these labourers was to generate wealth for the nation – not raise themselves above subsistence. The rights of the individual were subservient to those of the state.

To maximize efficiency, European governments micro-managed the economy. Colbert famously ruled that fabrics from Dijon should contain exactly 1,408 threads.

Rational mechanics

Meanwhile, back in the universities, science was for the first time developing a viable, consistent alternative to the medieval worldview based on Aristotelian cosmology. Copernicus had shown that the Earth might not be the centre of the universe. Nearly a century and a half later, **Isaac Newton** (1643–1727) derived his laws of motion and the law of gravity in his *Principia Mathematica* (1687).

The force that makes an object like an apple drop to the ground is the same as the force that makes a planet go around the Sun.

This is as powerful an insight as the Pythagorean discovery that music is governed by number.

toms

Newton, like Galileo, believed that matter was made up of "solid, massy, hard, impenetrable, movable particles" (i.e. atoms) and his laws of motion provided a "rational mechanics" that governed their behaviour. It followed, then, that the motion of anything could be predicted using mathematics.

Mad markets

At the age of 53, Newton accepted the position of Master of the Mint. He took his financial laws as seriously as his laws of physics, and sent several counterfeiters to the gallows.

Unfortunately, he found that the economy was less predictable than the motions of the stars and planets, and lost most of his fortune in the collapse of the "South Sea bubble" in 1720.

Light vs. darkness

Other thinkers extended the reductionist methodology to society or the economy, as part of a larger 17th- and 18th-century Enlightenment movement in philosophy and politics that provided the intellectual underpinnings of capitalism.

Philosophers such as **Thomas Hobbes** (1588–1679) and **John Locke** (1632–1704) argued that the universe is inherently rational and can be understood through reason combined with empirical* observation. But their vision of a rational society was sharply different from the rationality of the medieval Scholastics. Instead of a pristine and fixed social order that reflected the pre-ordained order of the cosmos, the thinkers of the Enlightenment saw society as a contractual truce between self-interested individuals, interacting like machines.

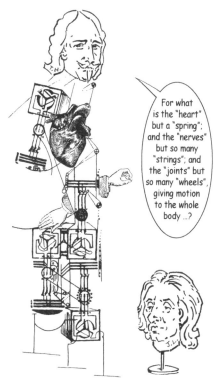

For what is the "heart" but a "spring"; and the "nerves" but so many "strings"; and the "joints" but so many "wheels", giving motion to the whole body ...?

* "Empirical" means based on experiment, observation or experience, rather than theory.

*L*eviathan

In his book *Leviathan* (1651), Hobbes imagined a pre-historical state without social bounds and constraints. In such a condition, mankind would exist in a "state of nature".

The life of man would be solitary, poor, nasty, brutish, and short.

← KING CHARLES II

To avoid this fate, people would prefer to submit to a supreme ruler, whom Hobbes calls the Leviathan.

In a world of atomistic individuals, the social pecking order was created solely by one person's power over another. The only stable arrangement was therefore to have a single strong ruler, as anything else would introduce division and discord (Hobbes was no doubt influenced by the outbreak of civil war in England, and the Thirty Years War in Germany).

Love of gain

Hobbes measured power in strictly economic terms.

The "value" or "worth" of a man is, as of all other things, his price; that is to say, so much as would be given for the use of his power ...

And as in other things, so in men, not the seller, but the buyer determines the price.

It followed that the Leviathan rules, not from divine right, but because of the consent of the people.

Leviathan was highly controversial and disruptive, but Hobbes was not alone in his somewhat sceptical and mechanistic view of humanity. And it soon became common to assume, as the Scottish philosopher **David Hume** (1711–76) later put it ...

... that people are motivated primarily by the "love of gain".

Locke's blank slate

The English philosopher John Locke was strongly influenced by scientists including Newton and the chemist Robert Boyle.

His *Essay Concerning Human Understanding* (1690) argued that we enter the world as equals, with our mind a blank slate.

We build up our internal picture of the world by learning rationally from sensations and experience.

It therefore followed that one's behaviour was a function of one's environment. Like inert particles, our trajectories depend on the forces we experience.

Unlike Hobbes, Locke believed that the natural state of man was idyllic, and in harmony with "natural law".

The social contract

Locke's *Two Treatises on Government* (1689) argued that the role of the state is to protect the rights and freedoms of its citizens. One of the key rights was property rights, which Locke believed are generated when people mix their labour with the material world.

The job of the government is not to assign these natural property rights, but to protect them. This is Locke's idea of the social contract.

The value of money

According to Locke, money obtained its value because, being made of precious metal, it could be hoarded without risk of spoiling. Society therefore gives its tacit agreement that money can be used as a medium for exchange.

Locke's work provided a political justification for the sanctity of private property and the accumulation of money. It later also served as one of the main influences on the constitution of the new American government in 1787.

One vs. plurality

Locke's ideas, and the growing emphasis on individualism, constituted a direct challenge to prevailing economic orthodoxy.

According to mercantilism, the aim of economic policy was to produce low-cost goods for export, and thus maximize the country's share of overall monetary wealth (which was assumed to be fixed). The system worked well for the state's elite, but less well for the emergent class of wealthy merchants.

The focus therefore shifted from the state to the individual, and from producers to consumers.

⑤upply and demand

Because mercantilists aimed to maximize exports, they favoured an artificially low exchange rate, which made goods cheaper to produce relative to those of other countries. But according to Locke's theory of natural law, money obtained its value from the consent of people and was therefore subject to the forces of supply and demand – as was the "natural" interest rate. If money was abundant, it would earn less interest than if it were scarce.

Interest rates should be set by market forces, not government regulation.

The face value of coins should also correspond to their intrinsic value in terms of precious metal.

This conflict came to a head in the 1690s silver crisis in England.

Silver crisis

English silver coins had become lighter over the years, because of the government's practice of "clipping" them – removing a tiny amount of metal from the edges, to be melted down and sold.

They therefore decided to issue new coins, but were unsure whether to restore them to their former level of silver (as favoured by Locke), or keep them at the new lower level (as favoured by mercantilists). Locke prevailed.

> But the unexpected result was that people hoarded the new coins and spent the old ones.

This is an example of "Gresham's law", named after the English financier **Sir Thomas Gresham** (1519–79), which states that "bad money drives out good".

Free trade

John Locke was far from being the only critic of mercantilism. **Dudley North** (1641–91) argued that trade was not a zero-sum game, but made everyone richer by promoting specialisation – just as Xenophon had observed in the Athenian city state.

The philosopher David Hume later pointed out that it was in any case impossible to maintain a constantly positive balance of trade. A surplus of exports would result in more money entering the country, which would increase money supply, which would cause inflation. Prices would rise, resulting in fewer exports.

The science of money

Placing the individual, instead of the Church or the state, at the centre of the economy was almost as revolutionary an idea as Copernicus's statement that the Earth goes round the Sun, rather than vice versa. Economics was no longer based on theology, but on scientific theories about human behaviour.

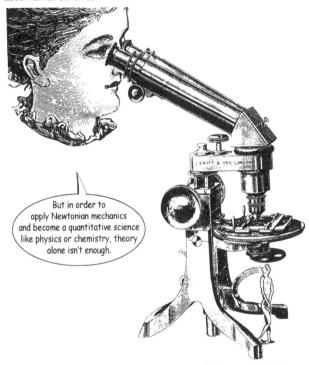

But in order to apply Newtonian mechanics and become a quantitative science like physics or chemistry, theory alone isn't enough.

Economists also needed to know what these individuals were actually doing. In other words, they needed empirical measurements of the sort provided by the English economist, inventor, philosopher, and enthusiastic gatherer of data, William Petty.

William Petty

William Petty (1623–87) studied medicine in Holland, worked for a time as personal secretary to Thomas Hobbes, then took a job as surveyor for Oliver Cromwell in Ireland. Because he was paid partly in land, he became a significant landowner there.

Returning to England, he became a charter member of the Royal Society (other members would include Locke, Newton, and other leading scientists of the day), and applied his surveying techniques to a survey of the economy. In works including *Political Arithmetick* (c. 1676), he tried to answer a pressing question:

Political arithmetick

Petty estimated that the total population of around 6 million spent on average £7 per year, for a total of £42 million. This expenditure had to match the total income from land, labour and capital.*

I estimate that £8 million of income comes from land rents (24 million acres at £0.33 per acre), and another £8 million from return on capital investments.

Land + Labour + Capital

It follows that labour must be responsible for the remaining £26 million.

Petty's next step was to assume that the three classes of assets – land, labour, and capital – shared the same rate of return on investment of 5 per cent. This implied that the total value of the labour force must be £520 million (in the sense that a 5 per cent return on that amount equals £26 million).

* "Capital" refers to resources that can be used for further production. Hence "capitalism".

Weights and measures

Because of the paucity of available hard data, Petty's work relied on some fairly heroic assumptions. But it was thoroughly in line with the Royal Society's programme to put science on a quantitative footing, and was a first step towards the type of detailed national accounting carried out today.

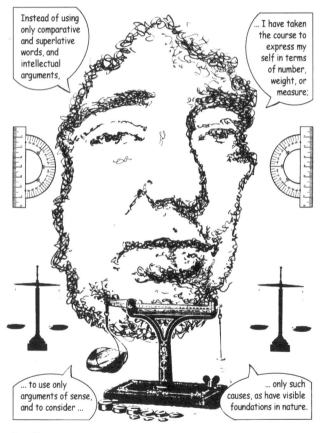

Making some dough

Petty's quantitative approach was taken further by his friend, the London draper **John Graunt** (1620–74). His work *Natural and Political Observations made upon the Bills of Mortality* compiled lists of births and deaths in London between 1604 and 1661, and can be seen as the beginning of the fields of sampling and demographics. Graunt used birth records to infer the number of women of child-bearing age, then extrapolated to the total population to obtain an estimated 384,000.

François Quesnay

In France under Louis XIV – aka the Sun King – Enlightenment values were kept in the shadows, but censorship was relaxed somewhat under Louis XV, leading to an explosion of scientific activity in the mid-1700s.

Like many other scientists of the time, including William Petty and John Locke, **François Quesnay** (1694–1774) received his university training in medicine. Locke served as personal physician to the Earl of Shaftesbury; Quesnay's job at the Palace of Versailles was physician to the mistress of Louis XV, Madame de Pompadour.

The Physiocrats

Quesnay's view of the economy was influenced by William Harvey's earlier discovery of the circulation of blood in the human body. Just as the body depends on the constantly recycled flow of blood, so the economy relies on the constant circulation of money.

And in the same way that the source of energy for the body is food, so Quesnay believed that the ultimate source of wealth is agriculture. All other economic activities were "sterile", meaning that they did not generate a surplus.

Together with the Marquis de Mirabeau and others, Quesnay formed a group known as the **Physiocrats** (the word "physiocracy" is from the Greek for "government of nature").

Le Zig-zag

With their own journals and textbook, the Physiocrats are considered to be the first properly organized group of economists.

In *Tableau économique*, first published in 1758, Quesnay showed how money flowed between the three classes of farmers, proprietors, and artisans, in the same mechanical way that blood flows between different organs. The table – an early version of what today is called a macroeconomic model – starts with an initial surplus generated by agriculture. This money is then traded back and forth between the other sectors.

Farmers pay rent to proprietors, who buy goods from artisans, who purchase food from farmers, and so on.

Even my closest followers became "bogged down in the zig-zag".

Blood-letting

By tracing these complex transactions through the course of a year, the table showed how the agricultural surplus was dispersed through the economy.

Quesnay's table was not just an abstract diagram, but was based on quantitative estimates of the real French economy. Quesnay also used this approach to compute the sensitivity of the economy to perturbations, such as the imposition of taxes.

The main problem discussed at Versailles was how to replenish the coffers of the French state so as to pay for the highly expensive Seven Years War (1756–63).

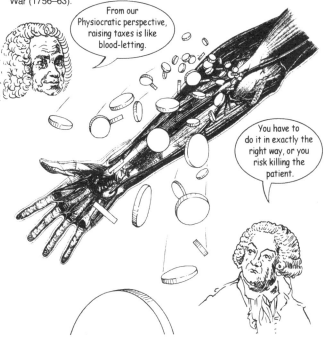

Go with the flow

Since wealth originated from the land, it followed that the simplest and least distorting way for the state to extract money would be a single tax on landowners, who did nothing but collect rent.

Given that the French economy at the time was governed by a complex web of taxes, subsidies, trade restrictions, price controls, guilds, monopolies, and so on, this proposal represented a radical reform.

Jacques Turgot

The Physiocrat programme was pursued to some extent by **Jacques Turgot** (1727–81), who served as minister of finance.

However, I soon ran into heated opposition from vested interests ...

... especially after he suggested that the corvée – a system of forced labour for peasants – be replaced by a tax on landowners.

Turgot

While the Physiocrats' ideas did not find fertile ground in pre-revolutionary France, their work established that theoretical models were necessary to understand policy decisions, and countered the mercantilist belief that wealth was due solely to advantageous exchange. Their *laissez-faire* approach also proved stimulating for a Scottish economist who stopped in on the Physiocrats during a visit to France: Adam Smith.

Adam Smith

Adam Smith (1723–90) is considered to be the founder of classical economics.* His main works were *The Theory of Moral Sentiments*, written in 1759 while employed as professor of moral philosophy at the University of Glasgow; and *The Wealth of Nations*, which he started while on a tour of Europe serving as a tutor.

The latter book was published in 1776, the same year as the American revolution. Along with Locke's concept of property rights, Smith's work would exert a profound influence on the constitution of the new government there.

At around the age of three, Smith was abducted by gypsies and held for some time before being rescued.

* Classical economics was a school of economics that stressed free competition and economic growth. It was succeeded by the more mathematical neoclassical economics in the late 19th century (see p. 97 onwards). Apart from Smith, key classical economists included Thomas Malthus (pp. 63–6), David Ricardo (pp. 70–3), and John Stuart Mill (pp. 74–7).

The Scottish Enlightenment

Smith was part of a movement known as the Scottish Enlightenment. His contemporaries included David Hume and Sir James Steuart, whose tract *An Inquiry into the Principles of Political Oeconomy* introduced the phrase "supply and demand" into English (though his unwieldy style meant the book was little read).

The group was characterized by their optimistic belief in the powers of reason, and their objective search for what Hume called "constant and universal principles of human nature".

At the same time, we saw human society as constantly evolving and progressing.

A good example was Scotland herself, which, as a result of the Enlightenment and the union with England, was being transformed from something of an intellectual backwater to one of the most advanced parts of Europe.

The age of commerce

According to Smith and other members of the Scottish Enlightenment, history had evolved in four stages:

> First, the Age of Hunters;

> ... secondly, the Age of Shepherds;

> ... thirdly, the Age of Agriculture;

> ... and fourthly, the Age of Commerce.

The exchange economy did not therefore arise out of a vacuum, but represented a confluence of political, judicial, and economic forces.

The government and the judiciary were necessary to establish and enforce laws. As Smith wrote in *Moral Sentiments*: "Society may subsist, though not in the most comfortable state, without beneficence; but the prevalence of injustice must utterly destroy it."

The mercenary society

The ability to feel sympathy for each other is important to grease the wheels of everyday life.

But Smith argued that the most essential thing that holds a society together, apart from a proper legal framework, is commerce.

A stable society can exist in which each person is motivated only by "a sense of utility, without any mutual love or affection".

And though no man in it should owe any obligation, or be bound in gratitude to any other, it may still be upheld by a mercenary exchange of good offices according to an agreed valuation.

*T*he Wealth of Nations

In *The Wealth of Nations*, Smith analysed – in language suitable for the general educated reader – the workings of the exchange economy, and asked how wealth was generated.

He criticized mercantilists for confusing wealth with the hoarding of money. As with anything else, the value of gold or silver depended on supply. An excess money supply would just create inflation. Smith therefore drew a distinction between **real** and **nominal** prices.

The same real price is always of the same value; but on account of the variations in the value of gold and silver, the same nominal price is sometimes of very different value.

The Author of the Wealth of Nations

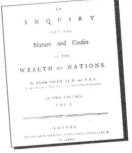

AN
INQUIRY
INTO THE
Nature and Causes
OF THE
WEALTH OF NATIONS.

By ADAM SMITH, LL.D. and F.R.S.

IN TWO VOLUMES.
VOL. I.

LONDON

A labour theory of value

The magic ingredient that determined the real value of an item was the **labour** necessary to obtain it.

> The real price of every thing, what every thing really costs to the man who wants to acquire it, is the toil and trouble of acquiring it.

According to Smith, this "labour" didn't only measure the human graft of production. In a modern economy, it also had to include factors such as rents or profits.

> In the price of corn, for example, one part pays the rent of the landlord, another pays the wages or maintenance of the labourers and labouring cattle employed in producing it, and the third pays the profit of the farmer.

The natural price

Of course, it was not possible to measure value except by comparison with something else, like money, so real values could only be inferred from the nominal price obtained in the market. This in turn would depend on supply and demand.

> If an item is in short supply, then its price will increase; while if there is a surplus, then its price will fall.

This led to Smith's key idea, which was that competitive markets would force prices to correspond to their "natural" level, defined as the equilibrium price at which the contributions of labour, land, and capital are all accorded their real value.

The law of economic gravity

In a competitive market, if a particular good were too expensive, then more suppliers would enter the market, supply would increase, and competition would drive the price down. If the price were too low, then suppliers would go broke or leave the market, and the price would go up.

The invisible hand

The beauty of free markets was that they achieved this feat without coercion or control or even deliberate intention. All they required to function was for people to follow their own desires.

It is not from the benevolence of the butcher, the brewer, or the baker, that we expect our dinner, but from their regard to their own interest.

By pursuing his own interest, the individual was thus "led by an invisible hand to promote an end which was no part of his intention". There was no conflict between self-interest and the social good. Capital accumulation was not a sin, but the source for investment and economic progress.

Market order

The invisible hand therefore explained in a single stroke how markets could align prices with "natural" prices; fairly distribute rewards for labour, land, and capital; match supply to demand, and so guide society to produce those items and services that are most needed; and self-regulate without the need for external interference.

> But some degree of market regulation is still necessary, for example to prevent the formation of monopolies, which will undermine the competitive mechanism.

Smith also saw a limited role for government in helping with public services such as roads and education.

Divide and conquer

Smith argued, like Xenophon before him, that a business can be made more efficient if its activity is broken down into many small tasks, with each person concentrating on one task only. He gave the example of a pin factory.

One man draws out the wire, another straights it, a third cuts it, a fourth points it, a fifth grinds it at the top for receiving the head ...

To make the head requires two or three distinct operations; to put it on is a peculiar business, to whiten the pins is another ...

The important business of making a pin is, in this manner, divided into about eighteen distinct operations.

Specialized tasks also lent themselves more easily to mechanisation.

Growing markets

The image of the factory also applied to society as a whole. The best way to promote economic growth was to increase the overall level of specialisation. This in turn would require ample amounts of capital, necessary to keep workers supplied with tools and machines; large markets where people could exchange their skills and wares; and free trade between nations.

The monopolies, tariffs, and closed-shop guilds that characterized mercantilism might appear on the surface to promote economic growth, but in fact they retarded it. In most cases, the best way for governments to optimize growth was to get out of the way (*laissez-faire*).

The Industrial Revolution

The concept of economic growth was relatively new, and would not have even occurred to people in medieval times, when social standing was determined by tradition or command, advertising was forbidden, and striving for advancement or riches was distinctly frowned upon.

But Smith's work coincided historically with the birth of the Industrial Revolution in Britain. The recent invention by his fellow Glaswegian James Watt of the rotary-motion steam engine meant that industries such as mining, weaving, milling, agriculture, manufacturing and transportation were being radically restructured.

Thomas Malthus

Enlightenment thinkers had a generally optimistic view of economic growth. For example, Smith argued that it would decrease child mortality (which in parts of Britain was over 50 per cent), thus leading to an expanding workforce. This in turn would keep wages in check.

The English curate and scholar **Thomas Malthus** (1766–1834), though, pointed out a potentially huge catch.

In America, families are reproducing at the rate of four surviving children per generation.

If this continues, the population will double in size every 25 years or so; and in two centuries it will expand by a factor of about 250.

In his 1798 *Essay on the Principle of Population*, Malthus argued that this could not carry on, for the simple reason that eventually people would run out of food.

*e*xponential growth

To demonstrate his point, Malthus used a minimalistic mathematical model.

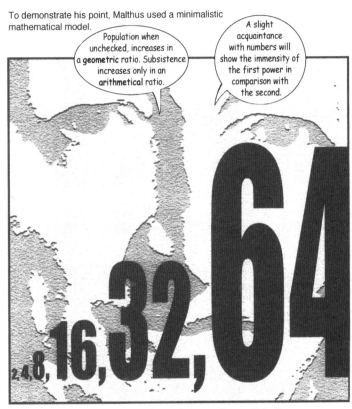

So if food supplies grow in a linear manner, they will eventually be overtaken by population, no matter how much food a country starts off with.

A "geometric" or exponential series is one that grows in a multiplicative fashion: 2, 4, 8, 16, 32 ... An "arithmetical" or linear series is one that grows additively: 2, 4, 6, 8, 10 ...

$\mathcal{S}$ickly season

Should the population become too big, nature would find ways to deal with it.

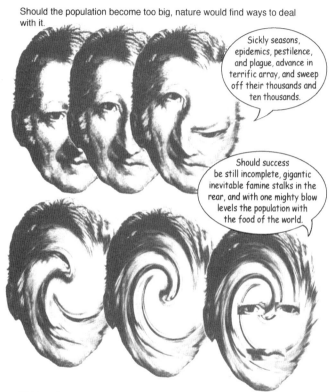

Sickly seasons, epidemics, pestilence, and plague, advance in terrific array, and sweep off their thousands and ten thousands.

Should success be still incomplete, gigantic inevitable famine stalks in the rear, and with one mighty blow levels the population with the food of the world.

Malthus therefore opposed the Poor Law, because it only encouraged the poor to have more children.

Malthus's somewhat gloomy tone was out of step with the expansionist mood of the times, and helped lead to economics being labelled by Thomas Carlyle as the "dismal science". Karl Marx later called Malthus's essay a "libel on the human race".

Survival of the fittest

Malthus's essay was a key influence on Charles Darwin's theory of natural selection and the study of ecological systems.

> Population pressures mean that only those best fitted to their environment ("the fittest") survive.

For human demographics, though, Malthus's calculations failed to take into account two things: the ability of technology to boost food production, and the relationship between wealth and fertility.

When a country gets richer, it initially experiences rapid population growth as the death rate falls – as in England and the US when Malthus was alive. However, this growth rate usually slows over time, because rich people tend to have fewer children.

Jeremy Bentham

A happier outlook on the economy was provided by the philosopher, jurist and social reformer **Jeremy Bentham** (1748–1832), whose **utilitarian** philosophy was to have a profound influence on future generations of economists.

In place of "natural law" of the type advocated by John Locke, or Christian morality, Bentham believed that laws and moral codes arose to meet the evolving needs of society, and should be designed according to the "greatest happiness principle" – i.e. they should provide the "greatest happiness of the greatest number".

Among my other achievements, I invented the words "maximize" and "minimize".

Similarly, the aim of the economy should be to maximize societal happiness.

The hedonistic science

"Utility" was defined as that which appears to "augment or diminish the happiness of the party whose interest is in question". It could be calculated according to the pseudo-Newtonian "hedonistic calculus".

Sum up all the values of all the pleasures on the one side, and those of all the pains on the other.

The balance, if it be on the side of pleasure, will give the good tendency of the act upon the whole, with respect to the interests of that individual person; if on the side of pain, the bad tendency of it upon the whole.

Rational society

Bentham's aim was to make social policy rational and enlightened. "Nature has placed mankind under the governance of two sovereign masters – pain and pleasure … The principle of utility recognizes this subjection, and assumes it for the foundation of that system, the object of which is to rear the fabric of felicity by the hands of reason and of law."

When he died in 1832, one of the terms of his will was that his mummified body would be displayed in a glass case in University College London, his head replaced with a wax copy.

BENTHAM'S POORLY-EMBALMED HEAD, UCL, LONDON

David Ricardo

Bentham's followers included the political economists **David Ricardo** (1772–1823) and John Stuart Mill (see pp. 74–7). They aimed to put economics on a similarly logical and utilitarian basis.

David Ricardo initially worked as a stockbroker, but maximized his utility and retired very rich at the age of 41 after betting against Napoleon in the battle of Waterloo (he bought British securities). He then served as a Member of Parliament.

In his *Principles of Political Economy and Taxation* (1817), Ricardo developed an economic theory that combined a labour theory of value (see pp. 33, 55) with some of the ideas on population growth of his friend and intellectual sparring partner, Malthus.

Rent is determined not by the value of land, but by differences in the value of land.

High rent

Following the Napoleonic Wars, the price of corn (which referred to cereal crops in general) in England was kept high through a mercantilist system of import tariffs known as the Corn Laws. Bread cost almost half a labourer's wages, and landowners were raking in profits (which was strange since they performed no labour).

Ricardo analysed this situation in abstract terms by considering the case of a growing population, which as it expands is forced to cultivate new land to grow corn.

Repealing the Corn Laws

Corn supplies will increase, which (following Malthus) generates further population growth. Wages go up to keep pace with the resulting inflation. Eventually, industrial profits decline, new investment ceases, and the economy reaches a steady state of no growth. Workers will be making more money in nominal terms, but their real wages remain stuck at subsistence levels. The only winners are the landlords, who passively benefit from the mechanistic effects of market forces.

The interest of the landlords is always opposed to the interest of every other class in the community.

There was only one way to avoid this stagnation: import corn. This would cut into the profits earned by landowners. Ricardo therefore advocated repealing the Corn Laws, and adopting free trade.

Comparative advantage

Ricardo's theory of **comparative advantage**, which showed how free trade boosted economic growth, was illustrated with a simple example: two countries, Portugal and England, trading two products, wine and cloth. He demonstrated that each country would benefit if it concentrated only on manufacturing whichever good it could produce more cheaply, and importing the other. Free trade was therefore much more than a zero-sum game.

In fact it is difficult to say where the limit is at which you would cease to accumulate wealth.

Ricardo's simplified analysis ignored many complicating factors – Joseph Schumpeter (see pp. 123–5) later defined the "Ricardian Vice" as the practice of choosing assumptions that give the desired result. But it set new standards for deductive logic in economics, and inspired future thinkers from Karl Marx to modern free-traders.

John Stuart Mill

John Stuart Mill (1806–73) was the eldest son of James Mill, a close friend of Jeremy Bentham. He was brought up in a hot-house of rational enlightenment, learning Greek at the age of three, Latin at eight, and Adam Smith and David Ricardo at thirteen.

At sixteen he discovered utilitarianism, which supplied him with "a creed, a doctrine, a philosophy; in one among the best senses of the word, a religion". At the age of twenty he went through a spell of severe depression; but recovered to develop his own form of political economics that merged utilitarianism and Ricardian economics in a new way. His *Principles of Political Economy* (1848) would become the leading economics textbook of his day.

$\mathcal{S}$pread the wealth

Mill argued that wealth *production* was driven largely by physical constraints and laws, such as the amount of land available for agriculture; but wealth *distribution* was more flexible, and controlled by social laws and customs.

The current distribution was "almost in an inverse ratio to the labour":

... the largest portions to those who have never worked at all ...

... the remuneration dwindling as the work grows harder and more disagreeable ...

... until the most fatiguing and exhausting bodily labour cannot count with certainty on being able to earn even the necessaries of life.

The role of the state should therefore be to design institutions that protect personal freedom (essential to maximize utility) but also support fair and equitable distribution – for example through inheritance tax, and profit-sharing arrangements for workers.

Human improvement

Mill was a committed social reformer, who saw the economy as more than the passive result of mechanistic economic laws. While Malthus and Ricardo thought the working classes would remain trapped in subsistence by their tendency to produce more children in response to any salary increase, Mill believed their behaviour could be modified through education about birth control and the benefits of small families.

In *The Subjection of Women* (written 1861, published 1869), Mill wrote:

The legal subordination of one sex to another - is wrong in itself, and now one of the chief hindrances to human improvement.

He also realized that economic growth and expanding populations caused damage to the environment, which itself was a form of disutility.

Steady state

Like Ricardo, Mill believed that society would evolve towards a steady state, with capital and population reaching roughly stable levels. However, he saw this in more positive terms than Ricardo. Instead of representing an end to progress, it would just be progress of a different type.

There would be as much scope as ever for all kinds of mental culture, and moral and social progress; as much room for improving the Art of Living and much more likelihood of its being improved, when minds cease to be engrossed by the art of getting on.

Mill was writing at a time when some of the unpleasant side-effects of industrialisation were becoming obvious.

Making money

Not all Victorians were enamoured by disruptive technological change, urban crowding, pollution from coal-burning, the emphasis on brutal competition, or the often terrible working conditions, in which factory work weeks could be 80 hours or longer.

In *The Condition of the Working Class in England in 1844*, a 24-year-old *bon vivant* from a wealthy German family, **Friedrich Engels** (1820–95), who was slumming it in Manchester, wrote a seething critique of English capitalism.

It is utterly indifferent to the English bourgeois whether his working-men starve or not, if only he makes money. All the conditions of life are measured by money, and what brings no money is nonsense, unpractical, idealistic bosh.

Some say I was the first champagne socialist.

Karl Marx

Engels's friend, the German philosopher, historian and economist **Karl Marx** (1818–83) believed that these mounting social injustices were an inherent feature of capitalism that would eventually lead to its downfall.

Classical economists from Smith to Mill saw the economy as consisting of atomistic individuals, all in competition with each other, and divided into the classes of labourers, landlords, and capitalists. Marx simplified this to two main protagonists: workers (the proletariat) versus capitalists. The former have no wealth apart from their labour, while the latter earn a return on property.

Because capitalists own the means of production, and have the cash reserves to outlast labourers in negotiations, they can dictate wages and working conditions.

(Marx and Engels, The Communist Manifesto, 1848)

The history of all hitherto existing society is the history of class struggles.

Surplus value

While classical economists saw labour as the ultimate source of value, Marx observed that this value was not fairly distributed, for there was a gap between the value produced by labourers and the wages they received. This "surplus value" represented the profit extracted by the capitalist – aka "Mr Moneybags".

In *Das Kapital* (first volume published in 1867, posthumously completed by Engels in 1885 and 1894), Marx argued that the imbalance in power between capitalists and the working class meant that labour would always be treated as a commodity to be exploited.

Boom and bust

Marx was one of the first economists to give a detailed analysis of the boom/bust business cycle. He argued that it was a consequence of the central drive of capitalism, which was to accumulate capital and invest it in labour-saving machinery. This process would after a time create a glut of production, leading to a crisis in which some businesses went broke (most classical economists including Ricardo thought that a general glut could never happen, because demand was essentially unlimited). Once prices and output were sufficently depressed, demand would be restored, and the cycle would start again.

The addiction to growth meant that capitalistic societies could never be satisfied with Mill's steady state.

Accumulate, accumulate! That is Moses and the prophets! *

* 'Das Kapital'

Class revolt

Marx estimated the period of the cycle at about ten years. However, the business cycle was just one component of a larger historical pattern.

Marx believed that the "immanent laws" of capitalism meant that with each period of boom and bust, capital would become increasingly centralized in the hands of a few. Industrial output would grow, but so would the exploitation and alienation of the workers. Lack of social mobility would mean that the gulf between workers and capitalists grew, until it eventually resulted in "the revolt of the working class":

... a class always increasing in numbers, and disciplined, united, organized by the very mechanism of the process of capitalist production itself.

The knell of capitalist private property sounds. The expropriators are expropriated.

The end of history

Following the **dialectical** approach of philosopher **Georg Hegel** (1770–1831), in which the struggle between opposing ideas leads to a synthesis and a new stage of history, Marx saw capitalism as only one stage in a mechanistic historical process. Just as the slave-based societies of ancient Greece and Rome gave way to feudalism, and feudalism yielded to capitalism, so the tension between workers and owners under capitalism would inevitably cause it to collapse and be replaced by a new classless state that represented the perfection of society and the end of history – communism.

Just as Darwin discovered the law of evolution in organic nature, so Marx discovered the law of evolution in human history.*

[*Engels at Marx's burial service]

Say you want a revolution

When the communist revolution failed to arrive on time, some (including Lenin) attributed the delay to imperialism, which temporarily extended the exploitable pool of labour.

But at the same time that Marx was ensconced in the Reading Room at the British Museum, working on revolutionary communist tracts, a different type of revolution was under way in the field of economics that would have an even greater impact on the way people think about money.

Economics was becoming an increasingly specialized and scientific discipline that modelled itself after Newtonian physics.

Rather than debating abstract philosophical concepts like the meaning of value, or discussing long-term social dynamics, this new breed of economist wants to make hard numerical calculations about the economy.

Number is all.

PYTHAGORAS

Ⓢupply and demand

In France, the mathematician and economist **Antoine Augustin Cournot** (1801–77) analysed the price mechanism from a mathematical perspective. He first developed the idea of a demand curve.

> The demand for any good will usually decrease with the price, so a plot of demand versus price (or vice versa) will slope down.

Similarly, the supply of a good will usually increase with price. The point where the lines intersect represents an equilibrium between supply and demand. **Fleeming Jenkin** (1833–85), professor of engineering at the University of Edinburgh, illustrated the relationship between the two in his 1870 essay "On the Graphical Representation of Supply and Demand" (versions of his figure still appear in every introductory economics textbook). The concepts of supply and demand had been discussed for centuries, but now they were being expressed in formal, mathematical terms.

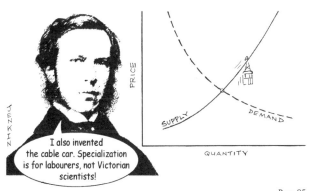

> I also invented the cable car. Specialization is for labourers, not Victorian scientists!

Real science

The English economist and polymath **William Stanley Jevons** (1835–82) went much further in mathematicizing economics. Reading works like Smith's *Wealth of Nations*, he was struck by the constant references to quantities and measures, and argued that it would be a small step to translate economic ideas into the more precise language of mathematics.

Now every use of the word **equal** or **equality** implies the existence of a mathematical equation; an equation is simply an equality; and every use of the word **proportion** implies a ratio expressible in the form of an equation.

Jevons believed that "if Economics is to be a real science at all, it must not deal merely with analogies; it must reason by real equations, like all the other sciences which have reached at all a systematic character".

Marginal utility

Jevons was a Benthamite, and believed that the purpose of economic exchange was to maximize individual utility – or more specifically, the **marginal utility**. This is the utility of the last unit consumed or produced, subject to the law of diminishing returns.

For example, a worker will continue to work until the pain (disutility) of the last hour of labour equals the pleasure (utility) gained from his hourly wage.

Pleasure and pain are undoubtedly the ultimate objects of the Calculus of Economics.

To satisfy our wants to the utmost with the least effort – to procure the greatest amount of what is desirable at the expense of the least that is undesirable – in other words, **to maximize pleasure**, is the problem of Economics.

REWARD FOR A JOB WELL DONE

Rational economics

By assuming utility maximisation, it was possible to build up a set of mathematical equations that govern exchange. For example, Jevons demonstrated that the ratio of prices for two goods would equal the ratio of their marginal utilities.

Jevons saw these calculus-based equations as the equivalent of Newtonian rational mechanics.

Market oscillations _____

Of course, utility could not be measured directly, but as Jevons pointed out, other areas including physics had the same problem.

For instance, gravity cannot be measured except by the velocity which it produces in a body in a given time.

In the same way, pleasure can be estimated indirectly by observing financial transactions.

In fact, economics had the advantage over other sciences in that there was a wealth of data available from the marketplace: "[W]e may estimate the equality or inequality of feelings by the decisions of the human mind ... and its oscillations are minutely registered in the price lists of the markets."

The average man

Another problem with computing or measuring the utility of a particular good was that it would obviously vary from one person to another. Also, price data was available only for aggregate transactions of large groups.

Jevons got around this by arguing that the economy could be understood by analysing it in terms of the "average man", a concept invented by the French scientist **Adolphe Quetelet** (1796–1874).

The greater the number of individuals observed, the more do peculiarities, whether physical or moral, become effaced, and allow the general facts to predominate, by which society exists and is preserved.

I deal markets _____

Like a physicist working on abstract problems in which effects like friction
are ignored, Jevons analysed only idealized markets, where information is
freely available and there is perfectly free competition
between participants.

He also assumed that competitive markets would drive prices to a state of
equilibrium. He compared the price mechanism to the motion of a
pendulum, which comes to rest at the ideal balance between supply
and demand.

This mathematical approach contrasted with the classical labour theory of
value, in which prices of goods reflect the labour of producing or acquiring
them, and neutralized Marx's exploitation claim.

Value depends
entirely upon utility.

Léon Walras

Jevons had focused on simple cases, such as the price of a single good. As Cournot noted, though, "the economic system is a whole of which all the parts are connected". For example, the price of wheat will affect the price of bread, which will affect the cost of living, which will affect the prices of other goods.

However, the French economist **Léon Walras** (1834–1910) decided to give it a go, and came up with a way to simulate markets for multiple goods.

Pure economics

In his book *Elements of Pure Economics* (1874), Walras analysed an imaginary market in which buyers and sellers traded a range of goods, and where producers could shift their resources from one product to another so as to maximize profits. Like Jevons, he assumed that markets were perfectly competitive, and that market participants would act rationally to maximize their utility.

The result was a complicated mathematical model, consisting of a set of equations that had to be satisfied simultaneously.

$$\Omega_b = F_b(p'_t, p'_p, p'_k, ..., \pi_b, \pi_c, \pi_d, ...),$$
$$\Omega_c = F_c(p'_t, p'_p, p'_k, ..., \pi_b, \pi_c, \pi_d, ...),$$
$$\Omega_d = F_d(p'_t, p'_p, p'_k, ..., \pi_b, \pi_c, \pi_d, ...), ...$$

$$\Omega'_b = F_b(p'_t, p'_p, p'_k, ..., P_b, \pi_c, \pi_d, ...),$$
$$\Omega'_c = F_c(p'_t, p'_p, p'_k, ..., \pi_b, P_c, \pi_d, ...),$$
$$\Omega'_d = F_d(p'_t, p'_p, p'_k, ..., \pi_b, \pi_c, P_d, ...), ...$$

$$p'_a = a_t p'_t + a_p p'_p + a_k p'_k + ...,$$

$$p'_b = b_t p'_t + ... + b_k p'_k + ...,$$

$$p'_c = c_t p'_t + ... + c_k p'_k + ...$$

> I cannot solve these equations myself. However, by counting the number of equations and the number of unknowns, I can show that a solution must exist.

He also argued, but never proved, that the solution should be stable.

The groping hand

While Adam Smith saw the marketplace in terms of an invisible hand, Walras thought more in terms of a groping process – or in French, *tâtonnement*.

He imagined an auctioneer who acted as an intermediary between buyers and sellers. The auctioneer would start off with an initial price, then adjust it until buyers and sellers were in agreement. The auctioneer therefore "groped" his way towards the price.

The final state of this process was the point at which demand perfectly balanced supply, and prices were at stable equilibrium.

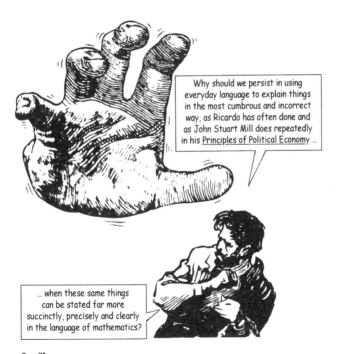

Why should we persist in using everyday language to explain things in the most cumbrous and incorrect way, as Ricardo has often done and as John Stuart Mill does repeatedly in his <u>Principles of Political Economy</u> …

… when these same things can be stated far more succinctly, precisely and clearly in the language of mathematics?

Vilfredo Pareto

When Walras retired from his position at the University of Lausanne, Switzerland, he was succeeded by his disciple, the Italian economist and sociologist **Vilfredo Pareto** (1848–1923).

I trained as an engineer – my thesis was entitled "The Fundamental Principles of Equilibrium in Solid Bodies" – and I also had experience in business and politics.

His 1906 *Manual of Political Economy* elaborated on Walrasian equilibrium and extended its mathematical base. It also introduced the idea of **Pareto optimality** (see p. 132), defined as a state in which any change that makes a person better off will reduce the wealth of someone else.

The 80-20 rule

Pareto is more famous today, though, for his empirical discovery of the so-called Pareto principle or **80-20 rule**. He observed that in a number of countries and regions for which he could obtain data, 20 per cent of the people held about 80 per cent of the wealth.

Furthermore, wealth followed a particular distribution, now known as a **power-law**, or **scale-free** distribution.

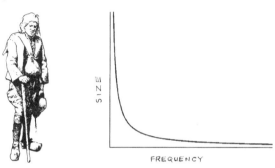

This means that there is no typical degree of wealth: most people have little money, but a few are fabulously rich.

Many natural phenomena are distributed in a similar way. For example, if you double the size of an earthquake, it becomes about four times rarer. In mathematical terms, earthquake frequency depends on size squared, or size to the power 2 (hence "power law").

Neoclassical economics

Together with other economists like **Francis Edgeworth** (1845–1926), Jevons, Walras and Pareto established the basis for what is now known as **neoclassical economics**. It still forms the core of orthodox theory taught around the world.

The theory drew an explicit comparison between economics and physics, for example by equating utility with the physics concept of energy; and it assumed, as Edgeworth put it in *Mathematical Psychics* (1881), that the actions of each person are directed to "realizing the maximum energy of pleasure, the Divine love of the universe". It also incorporated the idea of what came to be known as *Homo economicus*, or rational economic man.

$$0 = \left(\frac{dP}{dx}\right) dx + \left(\frac{dP}{dy}\right) dy + c \left\{ \left(\frac{dP}{dx}\right) dx + \left(\frac{dP}{dy}\right) dy - \theta^2 \right.$$

$$\left. \left[\left(\frac{d\Pi}{dx}\right) dx + \left(\frac{d\Pi}{dy}\right) dy \right] \right\}$$

where c is a constant;

$$\text{whence} \left(\frac{dP}{dx}\right) (1 + c) - c\theta^2 \left(\frac{d\Pi}{dx}\right) = 0$$

and

$$\left(\frac{dP}{dx}\right) (1 + c) - c\theta^2 \left(\frac{d\Pi}{dy}\right) = 0:$$

EQUATIONS FROM 'MATHEMATICAL PSYCHICS'

Rational economic man

The mathematical models used by the neoclassical economists all relied on certain simplifying assumptions about markets, such as perfect competition, and also about the behaviour of producers and consumers. The law of supply and demand, for example, required that people have fixed preferences for certain goods, which do not vary with time (since otherwise prices would not reach equilibrium). It was also assumed that people have access to all relevant information, and act rationally to maximize their own utility.

Thus was born rational economic man: the person who knows exactly what he wants, and acts rationally to get it.

The first principle of economics is that every agent is actuated only by self-interest.

t rest vs. in motion

The other key assumption of neoclassical economics was that the economy is drawn towards a state of steady equilibrium. As with the other assumptions, this was partly because it made computations easier. As Jevons wrote:

It is much more easy to determine the point at which a pendulum will come to rest than to calculate the velocity at which it will move when displaced from that point of rest.

And the same held for the economy. However, the assumption of stability was also necessary if the economy was to be seen as maximizing utility – since if it were in constant flux, then at some times it must be more optimal than at others.

The economy is rational and ordered, like the universe itself.

Pythagoras

unspots

The existence of an underlying equilibrium still allowed for random perturbations, or longer-term effects such as the business cycle.

Jevons had a theory that the business cycle was driven by sunspots.

Since sunspots affect the weather, which affects agriculture, which affects the rest of the economy ...

... it follows that the configurations of the planets may prove to be the remote causes of the greatest commercial disasters.

Unfortunately the average business cycle, which Jevons put at 10.5 years, didn't match perfectly with the sunspot cycle. This led him into a long argument with astronomers over the quality of their solar observations.

A specialized field

By the end of the 19th century, economists had largely succeeded in transforming their area from a branch of political philosophy to a specialized field with its own academic journals and university departments. The American Economic Association was founded in 1885, and the London School of Economics opened its doors in 1895.

With the neoclassical vision of a mechanistic world in which rational, independent, atomistic individuals interact like inert particles governed by fixed rules, economics was also becoming ever more mathematical – to the point where those without mathematical training were starting to feel excluded.

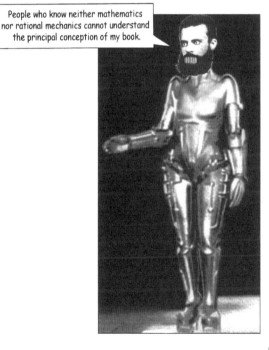

People who know neither mathematics nor rational mechanics cannot understand the principal conception of my book.

The neoclassical programme was further developed by the mathematician turned economist, **Alfred Marshall** (1842–1924). His 1890 *Principles of Economics* was widely used as a textbook as late as the 1950s. It did much to popularize ideas such as supply and demand and marginal utility, and introduced the concept of **price elasticity**.

> The elasticity (or responsiveness) of demand in a market is great or small according as the amount demanded increases much or little for a given fall in price, and diminishes much or little for a given rise in price.

In mathematical terms, the elasticity is inversely related to the slope of the demand curve.

> Calculus-based equations work because **Natura non facit saltum**: nature makes no sudden leaps.

Burn the mathematics _____

While Marshall used mathematics in his own work, he also insisted on the importance of explaining ideas using words. He described his method as follows:

(1) *Use mathematics as shorthand language, rather than as an engine of inquiry.*
(2) *Keep to them till you have done.*
(3) *Translate into English.*
(4) *Then illustrate by examples that are important in real life.*
(5) *Burn the mathematics.*
(6) *If you can't succeed in (4), burn (3). This I do often.*

Carl Menger

A separate strand of marginal utility theory was developed by **Carl Menger** (1840–1921) at the University of Vienna. He agreed with Walras and Jevons that utility is subject to the law of diminishing returns – the first apple to be eaten is more useful than the last. But he saw a good's utility as measuring, not pleasure, but its ability to satisfy human needs, which will vary from person to person.

Trade is beneficial because people exchange goods they have for something that they need more.

Middlemen are therefore very productive because they can match buyers and sellers who will both benefit from a trade.

Menger believed that economics needed to focus on the behaviour of individuals rather than groups or aggregates, because only individuals can act and make decisions.

One implication of his "subjective theory of value" was that individuals, rather than governments, are best able to decide what is good for them. Another was that economic theories are not testable in the way that physical theories are, because people are not inert objects. It is not possible to perform controlled scientific experiments on them without altering their behaviour.

Instead, economic principles have to be developed using a deductive approach.

The spontaneously emerging hand _____

Menger saw the economy in evolutionary terms, and argued that institutions, including private property and the monetary system, arise spontaneously as a solution to human needs, rather than requiring to be consciously designed or planned.

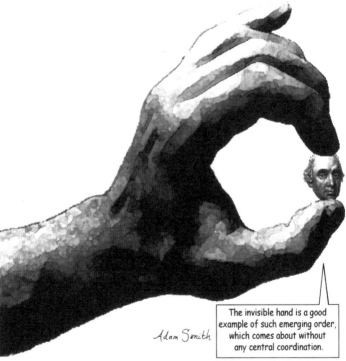

Adam Smith

The invisible hand is a good example of such emerging order, which comes about without any central coordination.

Menger's ideas would have a strong influence on a group that coalesced (spontaneously) around him, known as the **Austrian School**. Its followers would include Joseph Schumpeter and Friedrich von Hayek, who further developed the theory of spontaneous order, as discussed later (pp. 123–6).

John Bates Clark

Marginal utility theory also took root in the USA. In his 1899 work *The Distribution of Wealth*, **John Bates Clark** (1847–1938) developed a theory of marginal productivity, which argued that the wages earned by labour and the profits earned by capital equilibrate to their marginal contribution to output. "The distribution of income to society is controlled by a natural law … this law, if it worked without friction, would give to every agent of production the amount of wealth which that agent creates." Or more simply: in a competitive society, each gets what they deserve. The capitalist system was therefore the best way to distribute wealth. Clark was partly motivated by his dislike of communism, whose American followers he described as being of "worthless or criminal character".

Clark used the metaphor of an ocean to explain the marginalists' emphasis on long-term stability.

The surface, considering its size, shows only trifling irregularities.

If we take a birds' eye view … we may treat waves and currents as minor aberrations due to "disturbing causes".

Economies of scale

The neoclassical picture of stable markets, consisting of many small firms all in direct competition with one another, may have been mathematically tractable; but it did not conform very well to the situation in turn-of-the-century America, where giant companies like American Telephone and Telegraph, Heinz, Campbell Soup, Quaker Oats, Procter and Gamble, Eastman Kodak, and Westinghouse all exploited economies of scale to expand their reach.

Instead of the law of diminishing returns, it was the law of get biggest fastest. Monopolies and cartels were a constant problem, and railways used their position to control distribution and jack up freight charges.

Conspicuous consumption

The economy was dominated by tycoons like John D. Rockefeller (oil), J. Pierpont Morgan (banking), and Andrew Carnegie (steel), along with an expanding leisure class that asserted its status through what economist **Thorstein Veblen** (1857–1929) termed "conspicuous consumption". He observed that luxury goods could actually become more attractive the higher they were priced, which contradicted the neoclassical assumption of downward-sloping demand curves.

Veblen was a student of John Bates Clark, but rejected his marginalist theories in favour of a more anthropological view of the economy, known as **institutionalism**, which emphasized the role of accepted social norms and institutions. He analysed the rich the way an anthropologist might analyse the chiefs of an Amazonian tribe.

The leisure class

Veblen was something of an iconoclast who long found it hard to hold down a job. He wrote scathingly about both the rich and conventional economic theory. In his *Theory of the Leisure Class* (1899), he lampooned the utilitarian, equilibrium picture of rational economic man:

> The hedonistic conception of man is that of a lightning calculator of pleasures and pains who oscillates like a homogeneous globule of desire of happiness under the impulse of stimuli that shift him about the area, but leave him intact.

Veblen's successors included the Canadian-born **John Kenneth Galbraith** (1908 –2006), whose books drew attention to the cultural context of economic decisions, such as the way in which advertising shapes consumer preferences.

Irving Fisher

A drier and more conventional analysis of the economy was supplied by the mathematical economist **Irving Fisher** (1867–1947). The holder of the first Ph.D. in economics awarded by Yale University, he went on to develop or popularize many of the key ideas of modern economics.

The Fisher equation, for example, shows how to calculate the real interest rate r, taking into account inflation.

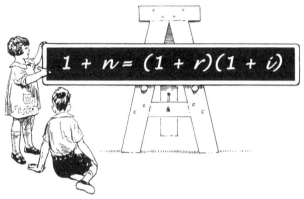

$$1 + n = (1 + r)(1 + i)$$

To a first approximation, $r = n - i$, where n is the nominal or observed interest rate, and i is the rate of inflation.

So if the nominal rate is 6 per cent ($n = 0.06$), but the expected inflation rate is 4 per cent ($i = 0.04$), then the real interest rate is only 2 per cent ($r = 0.02$).

Fisher

Quantity theory

Fisher also developed the **quantity theory of money**, based on the Fisher equation $MV = PT$. This states that the amount of money in circulation M, multiplied by the average rate (or velocity) at which the money changes hands V, is equal to the average transaction price P multiplied by the total volume of transactions T.

The left-hand side MV represents the flow of money through the economy – if a ten-dollar bill changes hands four times in a year, then it represents $40 in total transactions. The right-hand side PT, aggregated over a country, amounts to what today is called the Gross Domestic Product (GDP).

So the equation says that GDP equals money times velocity.

Fast money

This relationship is essentially an accounting statement, which was pointed out by other economists including William Petty. Fisher applied it by arguing that V and T are fixed with respect to the money supply, so if the supply of money is increased by, say, 5 per cent, then prices will also increase by 5 per cent.

The money supply can therefore be used as a lever to control inflation.

The Fisher equation has a clear analogue in physics, where an object's momentum P is equal to its mass M times its velocity V.

Newton

The Fisher equation formed the basis of **monetarism**, whose best known exponent was Milton Friedman (see p. 136).

Crash

Fisher was the most famous economist of his day, writing and lecturing on a variety of subjects including some unorthodox health cures, and he grew very wealthy. But his reputation, and his wealth, were damaged in the great stockmarket crash of 1929.

One week before the crash, Fisher said that ...

Stock prices have reached what looks like a permanently high plateau.

And he continued to reassure investors for some months that it was just a blip. The Dow index eventually lost 89 per cent of its value.

Fisher later warned, more accurately, that the Great Depression was being exacerbated by deflation, which had the effect of making debts even harder to pay off. By that time, though, people were looking to another celebrity economist for advice: John Maynard Keynes.

John Maynard Keynes

The Great Depression originated in the US but soon spread in a domino effect through industrialized countries as international debts were called in. In 1933, unemployment reached 25 per cent in several countries. The resulting social unrest helped bring the Nazi party to power in Germany.

John Maynard Keynes (1883–1946) had worked for the British government during the First World War, and represented Britain at the Versailles peace conference.

But I resigned because I believed the terms were too vindictive towards Germany.

I predicted, accurately, that the treaty would lead to financial instability and possibly another war.

In 1933 Keynes published *The Means to Prosperity*, which argued that unemployment could be reduced by counter-cyclical public spending (i.e. spending to boost the economy at times when the business cycle is in a downturn). This was followed by his magnum opus, *The General Theory of Employment, Interest and Money* (1936).

The paradox of thrift

The classical treatment for unemployment was to let wages go down until the demand for labour caught up with supply; and to cut back on spending to compensate for the fall in tax receipts. Keynes believed these policies were mistaken.

For one thing, wages are not very flexible, and are maintained by things like union contracts.

The paradox of thrift also means that during a recession, people save more and consume less, thus making the recession worse.

The economy could easily get trapped in a self-reinforcing equilibrium state of low demand and high unemployment, in which any extra money is hoarded rather than put to work or invested in machinery (contrary to Adam Smith's assumption). In the language of quantity theory, the velocity of money would slow.

The multiplier effect

The government therefore had to actively intervene, for example by spending money on public projects like railways. Keynes argued that this type of public spending also benefited from a multiplier effect.

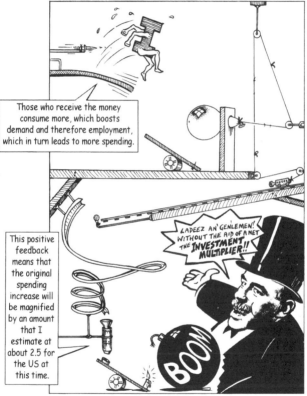

Those who receive the money consume more, which boosts demand and therefore employment, which in turn leads to more spending.

This positive feedback means that the original spending increase will be magnified by an amount that I estimate at about 2.5 for the US at this time.

Monetary policy, i.e. boosting money supply (see p. 137), would be less effective in a recession because the money would be saved rather than spent.

nimal spirits _____

Although he trained as a mathematician, Keynes was aware of the limitations of mathematical models, and the importance of psychological factors in propelling the economy.

Most, probably, of our decisions to do something positive ... can only be taken as the result of **animal spirits** – a spontaneous urge to action rather than inaction, and not as the outcome of a weighted average of quantitative benefits multiplied by quantitative probabilities.

Keynes's recommendation that governments should boost spending during times of recession was sharply at odds with the conventional view that the priority was to restore the financial balance sheet. That might make sense at the level of a single person, but not at the macroeconomic level of the country as a whole.

The long run

Keynesian economics, as it came to be known, also contradicted the neoclassical idea that economists should concern themselves with the long-term equilibrium, summed up by John Bates Clark's metaphor of a stable ocean in which recessions are only minor and temporary aberrations.

Instead, the economy had to be actively managed during recessions to maintain the correct relationship between employment, consumption, and investment (though this management could be relaxed when the economy was functioning smoothly).

This long run is a misleading guide to current affairs. In the long run we are all dead.

Economists set themselves too easy, too useless a task if in tempestuous seasons they can only tell us that when the storm is long past the ocean is flat again.

The New Deal_____

Keynes's ideas were controversial when they first came out, but they influenced, or at least helped justify, President Roosevelt's New Deal programme of public works designed to help pull the US out of recession.

What really revived the American economy, though, was the advent of the Second World War.

Economists played an important part in the war effort, in particular by using national income accounts to plan the enormous expansion in military procurement, while controlling inflation. This effort was led in the US by **Simon Kuznets** (1901–85).

The 1944 Bretton Woods conference saw the formation of the International Monetary Fund and the World Bank, along with the gold standard in which the exchange rates of major currencies were fixed to the price of gold.

These institutions, which were shaped in large part by Keynes, would play a major role in the relatively stable economic order that emerged after the Second World War. They were peopled by the many economists and statisticians who had been trained during the war.

> The success of national income accounts as a planning tool also led to the widespread use of the Gross Domestic Product (GDP), which I helped to develop.

> GDP sums the total economic activity in a country. But I didn't approve of its use as a measure of general welfare.

Kuznets

The business cycle _____

While Keynes's ideas dominated post-war economics, his interpretation of financial booms and busts – or how to handle them – was not the only one on offer.

As discussed earlier, Marx had a theory of the business cycle, with a period he estimated at ten years or so. William Stanley Jevons believed the cycle was driven by sunspots.

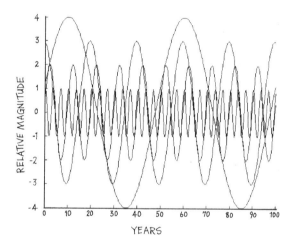

Graphical representation of the various business cycles overlapping; generated using overlapping sine waves with different periods, to correspond with different cycles. The waves in this panel correspond to cycles of 40 months, 10 years, 20 years, and 50 years. The panel on page 123 is the sum of all these waves.

The French economist **Clément Juglar** (1819–1905) argued for investment cycles of period eight to eleven years. In the 1920s, **Joseph Kitchin** (1861–1932) identified a shorter cycle of about 40 months corresponding to the time necessary for firms to build up inventory.

Some economists thought they could see longer cycles in the data too: there was the Kuznets infrastructural investment cycle, with period 15 to 25 years, and the Kondratiev technological wave that corresponded to historical patterns of expansion and depression, with a cycle of 45 to 60 years.

In his 1939 book *Business Cycles*, the Austrian School economist **Joseph Schumpeter** (1883–1950) proposed that economic fluctuations could be described as a composite of all these different cycles.

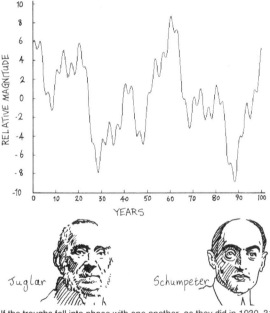

If the troughs fell into phase with one another, as they did in 1930–31, the result could be a catastrophic crash. (Today, though, most economists would side with Irving Fisher, who thought regular cycles were a statistical illusion.)

Creative destruction

As with the neoclassical economists, Schumpeter saw these waves as perturbations to an underlying Walrasian equilibrium (he described Léon Walras as the "greatest of all economists" and his system as "the Magna Carta of economic theory").

At equilibrium, Schumpeter argued that competitive forces will push profits down to zero, so investment will dry up. The agent that disturbs the equilibrium, and drives both profit-making and the development phase of economic cycles, is the entrepreneur – the talented person who comes up with brilliantly innovative business ideas.

The economy evolves because of the "creative destruction" that takes place during cycles.

Recessions are like a forest fire that clears away the old growth and makes room for the new.

Business cycles were therefore a largely internal or endogenous feature of the economy, an example of Menger's spontaneous order.

Hayek and the uncomputable _____

Friedrich von Hayek (1899–1992), who was based at the London School of Economics and later the University of Chicago, disagreed with both Schumpeter and Keynes, in that he believed business cycles were not endogenous, but caused instead by a mismatch between the "natural" interest rate and the actual rate in force.

If the government lowered interest rates artificially, then it might help sustain a boom, but it would also make the eventual recession even worse. The main problem was one of computability: the economy was too complex to predict.

The curious task of economics is to demonstrate to men how little they really know about what they imagine they can design.

So well-intended, paternalistic government policies will always be out of step with the economy. The best they can do is avoid interfering with it.

Hayek's influence _____

While Hayek was less influential in his time than Keynes, his work had a lasting impact on economists such as Milton Friedman (see p. 136). He later also inspired politicians including Margaret Thatcher, who at one Conservative party meeting held up a copy of Hayek's *The Constitution of Liberty* (1960), and announced:

This is what
we believe.

Meanwhile, other economists were finding ways to make Keynesian ideas mathematically consistent with mainstream neoclassical analysis. The result of their labours became known as the **neoclassical synthesis**.

The neoclassical synthesis

A core element of the neoclassical synthesis was the IS-LM model, derived by British economist **John Hicks** (1904–89) and others, which attempted to sum up Keynesian economics in a single diagram.

The figure is analogous to that of supply and demand (see p. 85), but instead of price versus quantity it shows interest rate versus output (i.e. GDP).

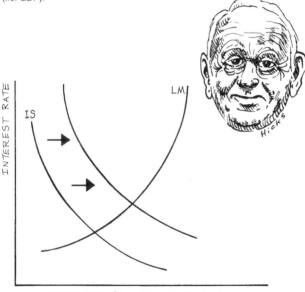

REAL GDP (Gross Domestic Product)

The LM curve (for liquidity and money supply) shows points that balance the money markets, while the IS curve shows points that balance investment with savings. The intersection of the two curves represents the stable equilibrium for the economy. An increase in government spending has the effect of shifting the IS curve to the right, so the equilibrium output is also higher, just as Keynes said.

The Phillips curve _____

The IS-LM model was augmented by the Phillips curve, named for the New Zealand-born economist **A.W. Phillips** (1914–75). This was an empirically-derived curve which appeared to show that unemployment and inflation were inversely related. Low unemployment – which can be viewed as a relative shortage of labour – was associated with inflation, caused by a higher price for labour. The curve was soon adopted by government planners as a policy tool to help avoid the extremes of high unemployment and high inflation.

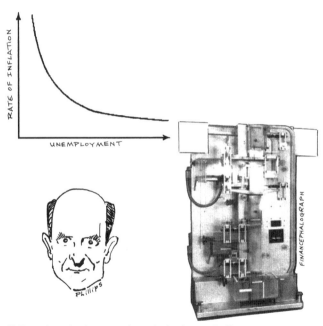

Philips, who trained as an engineer, is also famous for the Financephalograph, a physical model of the UK economy in which the flow of money between various sectors is represented by coloured water running through a system of tubes.

Paul Samuelson

The IS-LM model was popularized by the American economist **Paul Samuelson** (1915–2009), who incorporated it into his bestselling textbook *Economics* (first published 1948), which has sold over 4 million copies.

Samuelson's aim was to express the core economic theories in a self-consistent mathematical framework, based on two related principles: maximization and equilibrium.

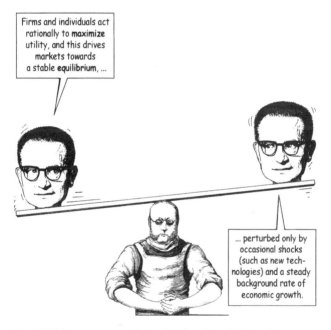

Firms and individuals act rationally to **maximize** utility, and this drives markets towards a stable **equilibrium**, ...

... perturbed only by occasional shocks (such as new technologies) and a steady background rate of economic growth.

The IS-LM figure was a way of extending these ideas to Keynesian macroeconomics – the economics of a country, region or the world as a whole. While the figure captured part of Keynes's argument, though, it also simplified it enormously.

Bastard Keynesianism

The IS-LM model took it as given that markets are at or near stable equilibrium, while Keynes saw the economy as going through sporadic mood-swings. It also ignored many of the complex and uncertain linkages in the economy, for example by assuming that the IS and LM curves are independent when in fact they may be closely related.

Hicks

Although I originally proposed the IS-LM figure, I later described it as a "classroom gadget" rather than a serious policy tool.

@?@*! KEYNESIANISM!

And the Phillips curve also broke down as more empirical data became available.

Joan Robinson

The English economist **Joan Robinson** (1903–83) famously called the neoclassical synthesis "bastard Keynesianism" because of the way in which it effectively neutered those ideas of Keynes that did not fit easily into the neoclassical mainstream.

Losing sight of uncertainty

Another aspect of Keynes's work to be lost in the wash was his scepticism of mathematical models, and his emphasis on uncertainty.

If we speak frankly, we have to admit that our basis of knowledge for estimating the yield ten years hence of a railway, a copper mine, a textile factory, the goodwill of a patent medicine, an Atlantic liner, a building in the City of London amounts to little and sometimes to nothing.

Instead, post-war economics was increasingly dominated by the use of complicated mathematical models. This had an effect on the type of questions that economists addressed. Issues such as social justice that had concerned classical economists like John Stuart Mill, but were hard to quantify, were dropped from the mainstream.

The Arrow–Debreu model

The ultimate example of this trend towards greater mathematisation was the Arrow–Debreu model, created by **Kenneth Arrow** (b. 1921) and **Gérard Debreu** (b. 1921) in the 1950s. It finally demonstrated the conjecture of Léon Walras that idealized market economies would have an equilibrium.

GOO-GOO GA-JOOB

©GRATUITOUS PUNS INC.

And furthermore it showed that the equilibrium would be Pareto-optimal ...

Arrow

Debreu

... in the sense that it is impossible to reallocate the goods without making at least one household worse off.

During the Cold War, the model was promoted as mathematical proof that the invisible hand of capitalism, and not the state fist of communism, was the best guide to organizing society.

hopping list

The basic components of the Arrow–Debreu model are lists of goods, firms, and households. Each firm has a set of production processes, which describes how the firm produces or consumes goods, and each household has a consumption plan, which reflects its preferences for the available goods (preferences are assumed to remain fixed).

Given a particular set of prices, the model computes the optimal consumption plan for households, and the optimal production process for firms. From those it determines the total demand for the available products at the specified price, and also the total supply from firms.

Future perfect

The achievement of Arrow and Debreu was to prove that there exists a Pareto-optimal equilibrium set of prices at which supply and demand balance.

To accomplish this feat, though, the model had to make many assumptions. These included perfect competition, perfect knowledge for market participants, and negligible transaction costs. But the strongest assumption was that market participants could rationally plan consumption so as to maximize their utility even in the future.

The jewel in the crown

This Apollo-like ability to look into the future was obviously very unrealistic. As Keynes had pointed out, our level of foresight is weak at best.

Nonetheless, the Arrow–Debreu model set the standard for mathematical modelling in economics, and soon became known as the jewel in the crown of neoclassical economics.

It also paved the way for the development of large Computable General Equilibrium (CGE) models, which are still used by policy-makers. These are similar in principle to the Arrow–Debreu model, but are simplified versions in that they aggregate over large groups of consumers and other sectors of the economy. They again assume an underlying equilibrium, rational utility-maximizing behaviour, and so on.

The powers of rational economic man exceed even my own.

Milton Friedman

The assumptions behind the neoclassical model had long been questioned by economists such as Thorstein Veblen, who mocked the idea of rational economic man, and argued that many aspects of social behaviour like conspicuous consumption were based on deep-seated irrationality.

The economist **Milton Friedman** (1912–2006) defended the neoclassical assumptions, however, by arguing that what counts is whether or not a theory can make accurate predictions.

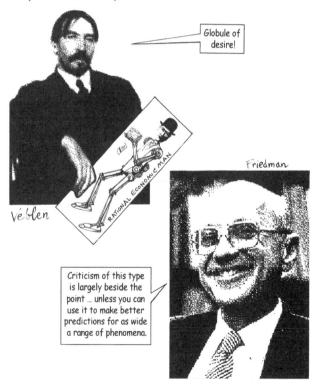

Globule of desire!

RATIONAL ECONOMIC MAN

Véblen

Friedman

Criticism of this type is largely beside the point ... unless you can use it to make better predictions for as wide a range of phenomena.

Monetarism

Friedman was a leader of the Chicago School of Economics, based at the University of Chicago, and is considered by many to be the most influential economist of the latter half of the 20th century. Perhaps his main contribution to economic thought relates to his work on **monetarism**. This theory is based on the Fisher equation: money supply times velocity equals price level times transactions (which in turn equals GDP). Friedman argued that the velocity is essentially constant, and excess money supply will feed directly into the price level.

Inflation is always and everywhere a **monetary** phenomenon.

The government's role in controlling the economy should therefore be limited to making sure that the supply of money smoothly tracks the GDP.

$\mathbf{S}$tagflation

Friedman's position therefore contrasted with that of Keynes, who believed that **fiscal policy** (i.e. spending government money) was necessary to combat recessions.

Friedman appeared to be vindicated by the appearance in industrialized countries of stagflation in the 1970s. This was an unprecedented combination of high unemployment and high inflation, which contradicted the Phillips curve and defied Keynesian treatment. In the US, the so-called misery index – the sum of unemployment and inflation rates – reached 21 per cent.

In the UK, the 1978-9 "winter of discontent" featured widespread strikes, with union leaders demanding higher pay agreements.

Friedman and others blamed this mess on Keynesian policies.

Slow and steady _____

According to the monetarists, government could not successfully micromanage the economy, because people would adapt their behaviour in a way that would neutralize it.

If the government attempts to prime the economy during a recession, say by lowering interest rates, then workers know by experience that over time this cheapening of money will lead to inflation.

They therefore react by demanding higher wages in advance.

The resulting inflation nullifies the policy action before it has time to take effect. The economy remains mired in stagflation.

The only long-term cure was for the government to enforce a strict and consistent monetary policy, with the money supply increasing at a steady rate in tandem with long-term economic growth.

Natural unemployment

Friedman therefore fought to replace active government intervention – which called for subjective political choices about how and where to spend money – with an impartial, apolitical, technocratic approach.

A monetary rule would insulate monetary policy both from arbitrary power of a small group of men not subject to control by the electorate and from the short-run pressures of partisan politics.

Friedman also argued that there is a "natural" rate of unemployment. Attempts to remove it would just boost inflation.

The Chicago approach

The Chicago School of Economics, led by Friedman, became famous for its free-market ideology, opposition to taxes, and visceral dislike of big government. Regulations were seen as inefficient impositions on the market. The role of the government should be limited to defence, justice, and basic legislation. Allocation of resources should be left wherever possible to businesses, not the state.

I even believe that the medical profession should be unregulated, and the need for doctors to obtain licences should be abolished.

Friedman served as economic advisor to Ronald Reagan and myself.

We applied our own versions of monetary therapy in an attempt to repair the US and UK economies.

Rational markets

These monetarist policies proved unsuccessful at controlling inflation and unemployment – the velocity of money turned out to be more variable than thought – and were soon abandoned in favour of a more active approach, which combined fiscal and monetary tools. Friedman too later distanced himself from monetarism.

> The use of quantity of money as a target has not been a success.

ALL-SEEING EYE ON THE BACK OF U.S. ONE DOLLAR BILL.

This didn't stop economics from coming to be dominated by the Chicago School paradigms of "rational expectations" and "efficient markets". The first asserted that people's expectations for the future are on average correct. The second went even further, and turned the financial markets into a kind of all-seeing god.

Perfect model

The theory of rational expectations was championed by **Robert Lucas** (b. 1937). According to this theory, people are not just rational, but also have a perfect mental model of the economy, in the sense that they don't make systematic errors. Markets have to be at equilibrium, because disequilibrium can be caused only by irrational behaviour.

These ideas could also be extended into other areas. For example, **Gary Becker** (b. 1930) argued that criminals commit crimes because they rationally play off the benefits of the crime against the dangers of getting caught.

Efficient markets

The efficient market hypothesis was proposed in 1965 by **Eugene Fama** (b. 1939). Echoing William Stanley Jevons (see pp. 86–91), Fama defined an efficient market as:

A market where there are large numbers of rational profit maximizers actively competing, with each trying to predict future market values of individual securities, and where important current information is almost freely available to all participants.

Under these conditions, he argued, the market price for an asset would automatically adjust to reflect its "intrinsic value". Any deviations will be small and random. It follows that, in an efficient market, no investor can exploit price discrepancies based on fundamental analysis or any other method.

No one can beat the market.

Economic astrology

The idea that market prices vary randomly around an equilibrium went back to a 1900 Ph.D. thesis, "Théorie de la spéculation", by French mathematician **Louis Bachelier** (1870–1946). Fama backed it up with statistical data which appeared to show that price movements followed a "random walk" that was inherently unpredictable.

It was impossible to choose winning stocks by analysing the attributes of different companies because, he argued, all the necessary information had already been priced in by the market.

And any prediction based on charts or patterns in historical data is like that of the astrologer ... of no real value in stockmarket analysis.

Of course, this hasn't stopped both "chartists" and astrologers from running investment funds.

Bad forecast

While the efficient market hypothesis helped explain why stock-pickers got it wrong, it also provided a degree of cover for economists. Since the Second World War, enormous effort and resources had been poured into the development of sophisticated mathematical models, such as the Computable General Equilibrium models.

The availability of fast computers in the 1970s, together with increasing amounts of economic data, meant that these models rivalled those used by weather forecasters in size and complexity.

But their accuracy was essentially no better than random.

They were unable to predict, for example, the annual fluctuations in GDP growth of the sort produced by the business cycle.

The normal distribution

$$\frac{\partial S}{\partial S} = \frac{\partial^2 c}{\partial S'^2} \cdot r^{\bar{x}-n}$$

The poor track record of economic forecasting was consistent with the idea that markets are efficient, and therefore unpredictable, as Fama had said.

However, while the efficient market hypothesis ruled out accurate prediction of day-to-day market moves, economists could still in principle calculate the statistical likelihood of prices moving by a certain amount.

Following Fama's definition of an efficient market, asset price changes over time were assumed to be small, random and independent of one another. They could therefore be modelled by the statistical model known as the **normal distribution** (also called the bell curve).* The standard deviation of the curve, which is a measure of its width, could be used to express the asset's volatility.

* The word "normal" is from the Latin for T-square.

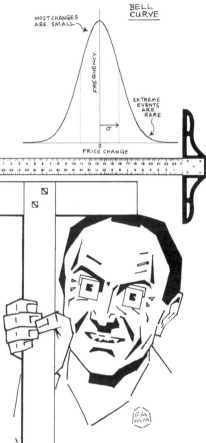

BELL CURVE

MOST CHANGES ARE SMALL

FREQUENCY

EXTREME EVENTS ARE RARE

σ

0

PRICE CHANGE

Financial engineering

$$\frac{\partial c}{\partial t} = \frac{\partial}{\partial t}te^{z}S^{z}, t)e^{-t(T-t)},$$

Because volatile assets like stocks are riskier to hold, in principle, than less volatile assets like cash, the standard deviation provided a method to quantify – and therefore control – risk. The field of financial engineering was born.

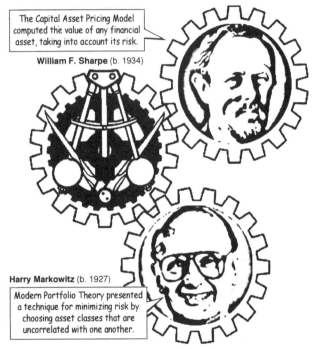

The Capital Asset Pricing Model computed the value of any financial asset, taking into account its risk.

William F. Sharpe (b. 1934)

Harry Markowitz (b. 1927)

Modern Portfolio Theory presented a technique for minimizing risk by choosing asset classes that are uncorrelated with one another.

In 1973, **Fischer Black** (1938–95) and **Myron Scholes** (b. 1941) came up with a technique for calculating the prices of options – financial "derivatives" that give one the right to buy or sell a security for a fixed price at some time in the future. The ability to consistently price derivatives greatly expanded their use – sometimes in destabilising ways, as during the 2008 subprime crisis (p. 169).

The Bank of Sweden Prize $= \frac{\partial c^{*}}{\partial t} e^{-rT-t)} \quad rS\frac{\partial c^{*}}{\partial S} + rc^{*} e^{-rT-t)}.$

The legitimacy of economics as a quantitative science was further advanced in 1969 when the Swedish national bank created the "Sveriges Riksbank Prize in Economic Sciences in Memory of Alfred Nobel". It soon became known as the Nobel Prize in Economics. Winners would include Paul Samuelson, John Hicks, Kenneth Arrow, Friedrich von Hayek, Simon Kuznets, Milton Friedman, Gérard Debreu, Robert Lucas, Gary Becker, William F. Sharpe, Harry Markowitz, and Myron Scholes.

The posthumous use of Alfred Nobel's name has proved controversial. It is now increasingly known as the Bank of Sweden Prize.

"Two thirds of the Bank's prizes in economics have gone to US economists of the Chicago School who create mathematical models to speculate in stock markets and options – the very opposite of the purposes of Alfred Nobel to improve the human condition."

Alfred Nobel's descendant, Peter Nobel, 2004

The late 1960s and early 1970s was a time of great optimism in science and technology. The spirit of the age was captured by the success of the moon missions.

Named for my reputed father, the god Apollo.

Economists were starting to believe that the growth of the economy could be predicted and controlled using equations, just as engineers could control the flight of a rocket to the moon. Economics became a growth industry, as demand from governments, private companies, and institutions like the World Bank and the International Monetary Fund exploded.

The period was also the height of the Cold War. The Russian defeat in the race to the moon symbolized the triumph of capitalism over communism.

Model economy $\frac{\partial c}{\partial S} = \frac{\partial}{\partial S}[c'(S^*,t)e^{-r(T-t)}] = \frac{\partial c'}{\partial S}e^{-r(T-t)} = \frac{\partial c'}{\partial S^*}\cdot\frac{\partial S^*}{\partial S}e^{-r(T-t)}$

Economics was also becoming increasingly abstract and mathematical. Human behaviour could be understood by "game theory" based on rational choice.

Classical economists had emphasized three sources of wealth – land, labour, and capital – with all their political and class implications; but now economists increasingly focused on the last two, and land was dropped from the list. Human ingenuity and technology could always provide a substitute, after all.

The world can, in effect, get along without natural resources.

Robert Solow (b. 1924), Bank of Sweden Prize-winner

Like a space rocket, economics could, it seemed, escape the bounds of the earth.

Earthrise

But while to many the moon missions symbolized man's triumph over unruly nature, another group of economists took home a different message.

The Apollo 8 mission of 1968 provided the first photograph of the entire globe viewed against the blackness of space. The "Earthrise" picture, of the earth rising over the moon's surface, has been described as the most influential environmental photograph ever taken. It helped inspire a new kind of economics that took the environment into account.

The vast loneliness is awe-inspiring and it makes you realize just what you have back there on earth.

ASTRONAUT JAMES LOVELL

Spaceship Earth

In his 1966 paper "The Economics of the Coming Spaceship Earth", **Kenneth Boulding** (1910–93) imagined the earth as "a single spaceship, without unlimited reserves of anything, either for extraction or pollution". He argued that mainstream economists still thought in terms of a "cowboy economy".

Like the pioneers who first settled the open plains of America, they see resources and pollution sinks as unlimited, and are concerned only with maximizing growth, as measured in terms of GDP.

In a world with limited resources, this was a dangerous policy, as the Reverend Malthus had pointed out nearly 200 years earlier. Boulding recommended a number of improvements, including replacing GDP with measures that account for resource depletion and environmental damage.

Nicholas Georgescu-Roegen

The Romanian-born mathematician and economist **Nicholas Georgescu-Roegen** (1906–94) argued that the idea of continuous economic growth, implicit in neoclassical economics, had the same problem as a perpetual motion machine.

> It violates basic laws of physics.

> Nothing can grow for ever without hitting fundamental constraints.

In fact, the entire mechanistic analogy was wrong: "[A]nyone who believes that he can draw a blueprint for the ecological salvation of the human species does not understand the law of evolution, or even of history – which is that of permanent struggle in continuously novel forms, not that of a predictable, controllable physico-chemical process, such as boiling an egg or launching a rocket to the moon."

Natural capital

The economic definition of value had to take into account not just human labour or ownership, but also natural capital. According to Georgescu-Roegen's protégé **Herman Daly** (b. 1938), much of what is called economic growth had already become uneconomic, once loss of natural capital was taken into account. The solution was to aim for what John Stuart Mill had called a steady-state economy, one that would keep economic activity within ecological limits, conserve resources for future generations, and focus on qualitative improvements instead of aggregate growth in size.

To control use of non-renewable resources like oil, in 1973 Daly proposed a cap–auction–trade system. The government would cap resource extraction, and sell the extraction rights to the highest bidder. It could thus control the rate at which resources are consumed.

Steady state

To be successful, a steady-state economy had to be organized according to different principles than a growth economy. Taxes should be aimed at "bads" like pollution instead of "goods" like salaries. Free trade would only encourage a "race to the bottom" in environmental standards (Ricardo's analysis of free trade, Daly pointed out, was no longer relevant in an era when capital was globally mobile and could dodge regulations).

Environmental sustainability should also be linked to social justice, because without it, a non-growth economy will create huge social tensions.

Steps such as minimum and maximum income caps might be necessary to reduce income inequality.

DALY

Ecological economics

The work of Boulding, Georgescu-Roegen, Daly and others helped found the field of ecological economics. Its central idea is that the human economy must be viewed as one part of a larger ecological system.

Economics should model itself less after engineering and physics, and more after the life sciences.

Rather than concentrating on abstract mathematical questions, it has to also address inherently fuzzy issues such as sustainable development and social justice.

While ecological economics gained in popularity along with the environmental movement in the 1970s, its ideas had only marginal impact on mainstream economics. But there were other critics of economic orthodoxy as well.

The church of economics

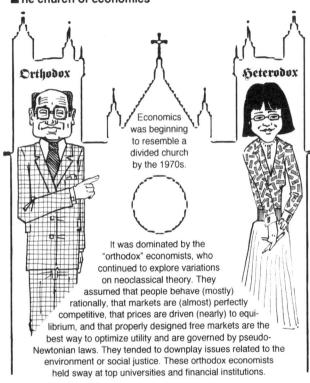

Orthodox

Economics was beginning to resemble a divided church by the 1970s.

It was dominated by the "orthodox" economists, who continued to explore variations on neoclassical theory. They assumed that people behave (mostly) rationally, that markets are (almost) perfectly competitive, that prices are driven (nearly) to equilibrium, and that properly designed free markets are the best way to optimize utility and are governed by pseudo-Newtonian laws. They tended to downplay issues related to the environment or social justice. These orthodox economists held sway at top universities and financial institutions.

Heterodox

Outside this mainstream core were arrayed – at varying degrees of distance – a number of "heterodox" branches. If this diverse group had one thing in common, it is that they disagreed with the basic assumptions of mainstream economics as articulated by US government economist **Lawrence Summers** (b. 1954):

Spread the truth - the laws of economics are like the laws of engineering. One set of laws works everywhere.

Behavioural economics

Starting in the 1970s, the Israeli psychologists **Daniel Kahneman** (b. 1934) and **Amos Tversky** (1937–96) tested the model of rational behaviour to destruction using techniques from cognitive psychology. Their work, which kick-started the field of behavioural economics, revealed many situations where people act less than rationally.

For example, we have an asymmetric attitude towards loss and gain – we fear the former more than we value the latter – so we often miss out on good opportunities.

We also dislike change, which explains why investors often find it hard to let go of under-performing shares.

Economists referred to this as "bounded rationality".

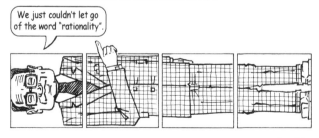

We just couldn't let go of the word "rationality".

Information asymmetry

Neoclassical economists like Jevons assumed perfect markets in which a large number of firms compete to sell identical products, and where everyone has perfect information. They therefore did not focus on the process of competition, in which a firm's size or market position matter, but only on the static and idealized end result.

In his 1970 paper "The Market for Lemons", **George Akerlof** (b. 1940) investigated what happens when not everyone has access to the same information.

There are both good and bad used cars (or "lemons").

If the true quality is known only to the seller, then the buyer's best guess will be that a given car is of average quality, and he will only be willing to pay an average price.

So the sellers of good-quality cars won't get a high enough price to make selling worthwhile. The "bads" will drive out the "goods" from the market.

Power law

While mainstream economics could just about accomodate things like "bounded rationality" or "asymmetric information" by tweaking its models, it was harder to explain the growing disparities of wealth between rich and poor.

In *The Theory of Moral Sentiments*, Adam Smith had argued that the invisible hand of the markets meant that the rich "divide with the poor the produce of all their improvements" in a fair way. Then in the 19th century, Vilfredo Pareto had demonstrated the 80-20 law, in which 20 per cent of the people had 80 per cent of the wealth. But starting around the 1970s, CEO pay in rich countries soared while median salaries stagnated, and billions around the world struggled to feed themselves.

Starvation is the characteristic of some people not having enough food to eat. It is not the characteristic of there being not enough food to eat.

Amartya Sen (b. 1933)

The science of happiness

According to neoclassical economics, the economy was a machine for creating what Francis Edgeworth called "the maximum energy of pleasure". But studies of self-reported life satisfaction showed that the pleasure machine was failing even in rich countries like the US, where happiness peaked some time back in the 1950s or 60s, and had been in slight decline ever since.

As Thorstein Veblen pointed out, resources are shifted from satisfying genuine needs to a futile arms race of conspicious consumption. Indeed, one of the main points of advertising and marketing is to make people unhappy with what they have – so they'll buy something new!

Feminist economics

Part of the problem, according to feminist economists, was that mainstream economic theory – and particularly the idea of rational economic man – was based on stereotypically "male" values such as competitiveness, individualism, and rationality.

Economics needs to take into account "softer" values such as social connectedness.

Women's contributions to "social capital" are undervalued. Society needs more than commerce in order to function.

A leader in this area was New Zealand politician and academic **Marilyn Waring** (b. 1952), whose 1988 book *Counting for Nothing* showed that GDP missed a huge amount of (largely female) unpaid labour, such as bearing children; bringing them up and educating them; looking after the weak, disabled, sick, or aged; and running the household.

The Minsky Moment

Another basic assumption of neoclassical economics that jarred somewhat with reality was that the economy is fundamentally stable. Even the business cycle could be explained as a rational response to temporary shocks, such as technological innovations, which perturb the steady state of the economy.

In his Financial Instability Hypothesis of 1992, American economist **Hyman Minsky** (1919–96) argued that the economy is instead prone to dangerous bubbles and crashes.

In prosperous times, debt accumulates in the economy as success breeds increasing confidence - Keynes's "animal spirits".

The process continues until it finally reaches a crisis point, now known as the Minsky Moment, when the debt gets called in and the economy crashes.

Crash-prone

There was plenty of historical evidence to back up Minsky's claim that the economy was crash-prone, going back at least to the Dutch tulip mania of 1637, when prices for the bulb bloomed to amazing heights before suddenly collapsing; or the South Sea bubble that had so assaulted Isaac Newton's retirement account.

The French-born mathematician **Benoît Mandelbrot** (1924–2010), better known for his work in fractals than finance, had argued since the early 1960s that economic data such as price changes do not follow a bell curve – as predicted by the efficient market hypothesis – but are better described by a power-law distribution, similar to that of earthquakes (see p. 96). Most price changes are small, but a small number are huge. This meant that risk analysis tools based on the bell curve dangerously underestimated the probability of extreme events like crashes.

It seems that nature does make sudden leaps after all.

Complex systems

At the same time that the assumptions of mainstream economics were coming under increasing scrutiny, new tools were being developed in other branches of science that would enable a different way of modelling and understanding the economy. These included:

Network theory. Studies the relationships between objects in complex networks, such as social networks, the World Wide Web, or the finance system.

Nonlinear dynamics. Studies how feedback loops affect dynamic systems such as the atmosphere, or a living cell. Rather than being at equilibrium, such systems are better described as "far from equilibrium" in the sense that their contents are constantly being churned around.

Complexity science. Studies complex systems, characterized by "emergent properties" that defy prediction and are resistant to a reductionist approach.

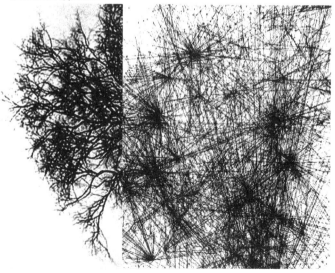

Agent-based models

Economists had touched on these areas before – for example, the Austrian School economists who argued that the economy is characterized by spontaneous or emergent order (see pp. 123–6). But new computational approaches meant that scientists could perform detailed simulations that went beyond simple mechanistic explanations or crude aggregate measures of supply, demand, velocity, and so on.

An example is agent-based models of an artificial stockmarket. Here the agents correspond to individual traders, whose behaviour is influenced by each other and the state of the market. Simulations can reproduce the emergent power-law behaviour of real markets, and explain why the invisible hand has a bad case of the shakes.

The law of supply and demand breaks down if supply influences demand, and vice versa.

Uncertainty reappears

The acid test of reductionist theory has traditionally been whether or not a new theory or technique can provide superior predictions. Newton's law of gravity was overthrown only when Einstein's relativistic theory proved more accurate.

In systems science, the situation is more complicated. The properties of complex organic systems – such as emergent properties and feedback loops – make them inherently difficult to predict. Models are seen only as imperfect patches.

Viewed from this perspective, the idea that rational economic man can accurately chart his future, let alone hold a perfect mental model of the entire economy, begins to seem less a scientific theory than a projection of abstract ideals – a modern version of the Harmony of the Spheres.

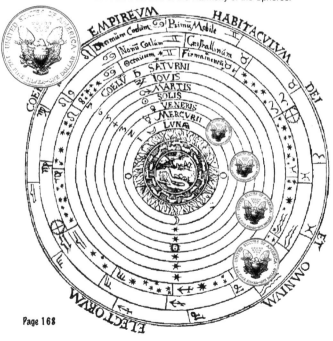

Subprime

Although tools like network theory and complexity were revolutionizing other areas of science, such as systems biology, they still failed to penetrate mainstream economics – in part because few economists had training in the appropriate types of mathematics.

Impetus for change picked up in the aftermath of the 2008 subprime mortgage and credit crisis, which resulted in trillions of dollars being wiped off global stockmarkets. Not only did the conventional mathematical models fail to predict the crisis – they also helped cause it, by underestimating the inherent risk in the economy.

The neoclassical image of the economy as stable, rational, and self-regulating turned out to be highly misleading. People from physicists to hedge fund managers demanded a new approach.

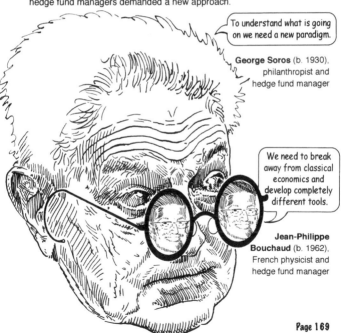

To understand what is going on we need a new paradigm.

George Soros (b. 1930), philanthropist and hedge fund manager

We need to break away from classical economics and develop completely different tools.

Jean-Philippe Bouchaud (b. 1962), French physicist and hedge fund manager

A lack of ethics

Perhaps the biggest shock from the subprime crisis, at least to the general public, was the behaviour exhibited by traders and institutions in the financial markets – from mortgage brokers who pushed people into signing contracts they didn't understand and couldn't hope to honour, to giant Wall Street firms like Goldman Sachs, who in 2010 were accused by US regulators of misleading investors.

By posing as an objective science, economics had seemed to remove the need for ethical decisions.

The emphasis put on ethics by Aristotle and the Scholastics had been wiped away by the Enlightenment – but it turned out that the invisible hand was not a satisfactory substitute.

Linear science

Science is often assumed to be a linear process of constant refinement and improvement. Until the late 1960s, economics could be viewed in this way.

The ideas of supply and demand, for example, were discussed by the ancients, elaborated on by the Scholastics, and led eventually to my idea of the invisible hand.

This was formalized by Walras, with his models of equilibrium, and finally "proved" subject to artificial constraints by the Arrow-Debreu model.

It was then expanded by the neoclassical synthesis to give a complete, self-consistent description of the economy – and even extended as a model of human behaviour to other areas of social science, such as criminology.

Post-Pythagorean economics

Indeed, mainstream economic theory can be viewed as the ultimate example of the mechanistic, reductionist approach to the world that goes back to the time of Pythagoras. Economists have done much to help understand and defend competitive markets, individual rights, and economic growth.

But a new kind of economics is now emerging that overthrows this ancient paradigm. Instead of analysing the ideal of rational economic man, it considers the behaviour of real people who are embedded in nonlinear dynamic networks. Instead of seeing the economy as a competition between disconnected individuals for scarce resources, it also considers the "softer" values of connectedness and sustainability.

LIMITED

ONE

MALE

STRAIGHT

AT REST

UNLIMITED

PLURALITY

FEMALE

CROOKED

IN MOTION

"*E*co-nomics"

Perhaps most importantly, the new economics places the human economy in its larger context, as part of the world system.

This is an exciting time in economics.

Further Reading

Roger E. Backhouse, *The Penguin History of Economics*, Penguin (2002)

Eric D. Beinhocker, *Origin of Wealth: Evolution, Complexity, and the Radical Remaking of Economics*, Harvard Business School Press (2006)

Todd Buchholz, *New Ideas from Dead Economists: An Introduction to Modern Economic Thought*, Penguin, rev'd edn (1999)

Herman E. Daly, *Beyond Growth: The Economics of Sustainable Development*, Beacon Press (1996)

Robert L. Heilbroner, *The Worldly Philosophers: The Lives, Times, and Ideas of the Great Economic Thinkers*, Penguin, 7th rev'd edn (2000)

Benoît B. Mandelbrot and Richard L. Hudson, *The (Mis)Behaviour of Markets: A Fractal View of Financial Turbulence*, Basic Books (2004)

David Orrell, *Economyths: Ten Ways That Economics Gets it Wrong*, Icon Books (2010)

Steven Pressman, *Fifty Major Economists*, Routledge, 2nd edn (2006)

David Orrell is an applied mathematician and author of several books including *Economyths*. Keep up with him online at www.davidorrell.com and www.facebook.com/economyths.

Acknowledgements
The author would like to thank Norbert Häring, Herman Daly and Beatriz Leon for their valuable comments on the text. He dedicates the book to Isabel.

Borin Van Loon is a surrealist artist, humourist and collagist. This is his sixteenth documentary comic book. He is also the creator of *The Bart Dickon Omnibus* and other books. www.borinvanloon.co.uk

Index

✂